Flyfishing
the Rockies

To my Father, Forrest and Al

Flyfishing the Rockies

By
William C. Black

PRUETT PUBLISHING COMPANY
Boulder, Colorado

Library of Congress Cataloging in Publication Data

Black, William C   1931-
  Flyfishing the Rockies.

  1. Fly fishing. 2. Trout fishing. 3. Fishing
— Rocky Mountains. I. Title.
SH456.B55   799.1'7'55   76-22572
ISBN 0-87108-507-0

First Edition

1 2 3 4 5 6 7 8 9 10

Printed in the United States of America

iv

INTRODUCTION

Shelves are already crowded with so many books on flyfishing that an author should really have an excuse before launching another. This contribution to the littered angling literature focuses on the Rockies, a region of unique interest to fishermen. The very character of most mountain streams is distinctive. Our rugged terrain includes a great deal of semivertical real estate such that streams tend to be swift, while boulders tumble from steep banks into streambeds creating a great deal of water detail. Happily, this situation makes the trout relatively easy to locate and reasonably difficult to frighten. Thus, anglers can afford to be a bit bolder and more direct in their dealings with their quarry than those who challenge the hallowed flyfishing shrines of the East.

Beyond this, the Rockies offer a truly remarkable number and diversity of trout waters, ranging from the big rivers and their tributaries down to myriads of smaller brooks. Of course, rivers such as the Madison are legendary, but plainer streams can provide adventure, too. For example, certain creeks that offer only put-and-take hatchery Rainbow along accessible lower reaches serve as bastions for colorful Cutthroat in their headwaters. In between, the stream may filter through impenetrable willow thickets and squirm past sheer-walled box canyons to finally open into a short meadow just below the snow banks from which it was born on the highest talus slopes at the valley's head. Scarcely a yard across and enclosed by undercut tundra and wild fllower banks, these rills sometimes conceal foot-long (or larger) Cutthroat, native inhabitants of a bygone era. There are rarely trails to such spots, the climb is always a steep one, and, for that matter, the whole venture often amounts to a gamble, since many headwaters contain only a few tiny trout. However, for many of us trips likes these are well worthwhile, for it's a thrill to realize that these wild places are as they were hundreds of years ago; a rare opportunity for an actual look into the past!

Then there are the placid beaver ponds, a study unto themselves; someone should write a book about the many angling angles they present. Here one year and washed out the next, beaver dams can be hard to find, reach, and fish, but they are often rich in fish foder and thus have potential for explosive trout growth.

There are quite literally thousands of lakes nestled within glacial cirques near timberline, spectacularly scenic settings almost without exception. The high lakes have a peculiarly compelling aura of primitive mystique, for while some are barren, other contain trophy trout within their inky depths. When clouds descend to engulf them, one may be "treated" to an awesome display of lightning combined with midsummer snow!

Adventure and esthetics aside, many of our waters are less than easily accessible, and some are just plain remote. As a consequence, angling pressure gets diluted. It has always seemed to me that our regional anglers have a special opportunity to "buy" good fishing. I don't mean by purchasing membership in a club with access to select water, but through expenditure of a little extra physical effort (often surprisingly little), perhaps combined with a little imagination and map-reading ingenuity. This is a pleasingly equitable situation consistent with one's romantic concept of how the wild west used to be or ought to be (and perhaps still is, at least in part).

The book's foundation is built from three kinds of information I've collected. Of course, I've compiled questions that have been asked at seminars. These are the things that beginners wonder about, and while the queries have been many, the same ones tend to come up again and again. Secondly, there are those questions that are *not* asked. Certain considerations which seem obvious enough to an experienced angler simply don't occur to the novice, for these are issues that become apparent only after one has put in some time on the water. Finally, there's no substitute for just watching new flyfishers in action. Interestingly, the problems and hang-ups (quite literally) that most beginners have are pretty much the same.

The book begins with four chapters concerning the tactical decisions that every angler must make during the course of a day on the stream. As we shall see, in time these thought processes become virtually subconscious, essentially forming the very substance of a fisherman's skill base. Certain mechanical steps are intimately blended with these tactics such that it is impossible to separate observation from thought from action.

It might seem more logical to begin by looking at equipment, but it's all too easy to get bogged down with tackle talk, and I prefer to think about what the gear is supposed to accomplish before worrying about individual pieces of equipment. When it comes to tackle, my strong bias is toward functional practicality with an eye toward the checkbook! As to artificial flies, it's rather surprising how far down the road one can get toward an understanding of what it takes to become a successful flyfisher without becoming preoccupied by fly patterns or even the basic differences between wet and dry flies. Comparisons between sinking and floating flies take on the proportions of a real war in the minds of some anglers; however, the real winner is determined more by the conditions at hand than by the fisherman's individual preference or prejudice. I firmly believe that *both* are best at one time or place, and that the purist who confines his fishing to one or the other must eventually suffer the consequences.

I have barely scratched the surface insofar as the study of insects pertinent to trout fishing is concerned — so-called stream-side entomology. While I'm far from an authority, I have achieved a highly profitable, if not casual, acquaintance with these many creatures. It is important to understand that one can enjoy many practical rewards from a fairly superficial knowledge in this area. There are several excellent and detailed books on trout-related entomology for those who wish to pursue the matter.

Angling anecdotes are scattered throughout the book to underscore or illustrate one point or another. These are "short" rather than long tales, largely devoid of drama or high excitement, for they actually took place! Events that occur in real life tend to be on the homely side, but are perhaps all the more believable? These experiences were generated on creeks, streams, and rivers from Idaho to New Mexico and constitute a set of angling lessons that has proven most valuable over the years.

Stream fishing is an action sport, and action things are learned by doing, not from books. Thus, our game plan is to provide the beginner with an idea base along the lines of how to proceed in hopes that his or her progress can be catalyzed and accelerated. Of course, there are shortcuts to be taken and pitfalls to be avoided, but I will be first to admit that in the final analysis most of us are essentially self-taught. Further, I suspect that many flyfishers really have the most fun *while* they are learning, a pretty good reason for taking up the sport, I think!

Table of Contents

WHY THE FLY?

Fly fishing a mountain trout stream is so much fun it should probably be illegal! If this is so, however, why are there so many bait and lure fishermen? After all, people recognize a good thing — and fly fishing has been around for centuries, plenty long enough for word to get around. I believe that fly fishing has an aura of sophistication about it, an exclusive image, that is somewhat intimidating. The tackle seems complicated and looks costly, and fly casting is supposed to be quite difficult. Many believe that in order to be successful, an angler must learn everything there is to know about insect life along the stream, and then fly fishing becomes more science than sport. Meanwhile, spin fishing has gained tremendous popularity during the past 25 years, for this kind of tackle is easy to understand and use, and it can be quite inexpensive. Spinning gear is much more widely merchandised than fly-fishing equipment (many mammoth chain stores don't carry flies at all), and so as a consequence, most new trout fishermen start out with a spin rig. The crux is that while spinning is ideal for baits and lures, it is an awkward means of presenting flies, particularly in a stream. Hence, spin fishers are seldom fly fishers; it's as simple as that!

I'm a teacher and have spent most of my life in the Rocky Mountain region. I've met countless newcomers to the West who want to give trout fishing a try. Students who would feel uncomfortable about coming in to discuss course work, tests (or even grades), frequently drop by for some casual trout talk. There is truly a remarkable grass roots interest in the sport. A number of years ago, I began to give informal seminars for students, faculty, their friends, spouses, kids, or just anyone who wanted to attend. My intention was to simplify fly fishing in hopes that they would give it a try and also to get them off to a fast, productive start. This book is based on those approaches which have proven most effective.

It's not that spin fishers are undesirable members of society, or that spinning is necessarily a poor way to catch trout. Rather than using such terms as "good" or "bad," I think of spin and fly casting as fundamentally different means of accomplishing the same end. The mechanics are certainly dissimilar. The fly rod is sprung by and throws a heavy line which pulls the leader and fly along behind in passive fashion while a spin rod is activated by the weight of a lure which it throws in the manner of a projectile. In spinning, it is the gossamer monofilament line that comes along for the ride, and a long one it may be at that. Spin casting in fact offers several advantages over fly casting, one of which is distance potential. Using spinning gear, any novice can soon learn to flick his lure a good hundred feet with no backcast worries, while fly rod casts of 60 feet or so begin to become something of a chore. Secondly, fly rods and heavy lures or baits just don't get along very well. The fly line and lure tend to go off in somewhat different directions, with resultant loss of both accuracy and distance, not to mention the possibility that the hook may end up in the back of the caster's neck! However, the very same bait or lure would be an ideal projectile for a spinning rod, actually increasing distance potential. It follows that spinning is ideal for ponds and lakes where hefty baits and lures are effective, and long casts are desirable. One simply throws way out toward the middle and reels back in. Spinning is essentially a means of trolling without a boat!

I have a strong preference for angling in streams as opposed to lakes, although our spectacular high mountain lakes do constitute an inviting fishery. Aside from the trout, these trips are invariably scenic, and sometimes exciting too, from the standpoint of lost trails, cliffs and snowbanks to be negotiated, violent storms, rockslides, and the like. However, there is a "feast or famine" aspect to fishing the deep glacial pools up among the clouds. On occasion, the trout are so eager that there's just no challenge. They'll hit anything from bare hooks to bobbers to apple cores; but at other times—totally unpredictable—one finds fishing so slow that no one has any luck. On those somber days, there's nothing to do but circle around and around the shore, casting and retrieving in endless frustration. A stream, no matter how large or small, has infinitely more interest and "personality" than a body of standing water. In the process of following the course of a stream, one finds ever-changing patterns of depth and current, of bank and bottom detail, all woven into a complicated and intriguing picture. It's like comparing a dull portrait with an action-packed movie! There's just more to see, think about, and do along a stream. Here the angler has a great many options for tactics that may improve his luck. It's the thinking man's game, so to speak, and correspondingly requires more know-how, including a variety of skills for which lake fishermen have no need. Of course, there is no need to limit one's fishing to lake or stream, but for sheer angling enjoyment and satisfaction, I'll take even the smallest brook over still water.

So why not spin fish a stream with flies? Since a fly is far too light to spring the most supple rod, it can't function as a projectile, and therefore some form of weight such as split shot or a plastic bubble must be added to the end of the monofilament line. Of course, the rod throws this ballast rather than the fly, and so it's the weight that lands where the cast is aimed — and often with a trout-terrifying splash! Thus the angler must cast off-target in hopes that his fly can eventually be brought into the water he wishes to fish. Adding weights so close to the fly also detracts from the terminal tackle's camouflage, but most bothersome of all is the necessity to reel the weight in almost to the rod tip before every cast. Despite multiplying pick-up ratios, the continual reeling is quite time consuming. By comparison, an angler armed with a fly rod has much more freedom and mobility. He sends the fly directly into his target, where it alights gently on a clean leader, free of bulky ballast. There's no need to touch the reel at all on most casts. A fly rod covers promising water on all sides in just a matter of seconds with ease and accuracy, a combination that's tough to beat! Nor does effective fly casting require exquisite coordination or years of experience, unless we are talking about hitting tiny targets from prodigious distances, as in an exhibition. Indeed, I've found that beginners can put their fly where they want it more easily with a fly rod than by spin casting, and significantly, most good fly fishers hook a majority of their trout at rather close range.

Cost is always a pertinent consideration, and as in any type of recreational equipment, there is a big difference between gear that will get the job done in perfectly adequate fashion and luxury tackle. I recently helped a friend get started with a complete outfit, right down to leader clippers and dry-fly oil, all for $46. Bargain-basement spin rigs may sell for under $15, but they are really no bargain; serious spin-fishers usually invest at least $50, especially in their reels and lures. In any event, fly fishing is by no means a sport reserved for the wealthy.

I've compared spinning with fly casting while avoiding the most basic issue of all. Which is the better means of catching trout, lures and bait or flies? There isn't a simple answer to this simple question because the winner will vary with the locale, time of season, weather and water conditions, insect activities — and, of course, with the skill of the competing anglers. However, in competent hands, the fly's won-and-lost record is impressive, for a very logical reason. When you think about it, flies selected to resemble insects upon which the trout are currently feeding must be more natural "baits" than flashing lures or hooks stuffed with kernels of corn or chunks of cheese. It's smart to have Mother Nature on your side, for she can be a potent ally and sometimes bestows her favors unexpectedly. One of the more decisive victories by an artificial fly I've seen found me on the wrong team! Oddly enough, the encounter took place on a high lake, a battle-ground where spinning lures ordinarily do quite well. It began one July morning as three of us slowly climbed the steep canyon wall of Middle Cottonwood Creek toward Ptarmigan Lake west of Buena Vista, Colorado. Our destination lay far above at 12,000 feet, nestled in a glacial cirque against a ridge of the imposing Collegiate Range between Mt. Yale and Mt. Princeton. It was tough going as we slashed through brakes of willows and skirted obstacle-course swaths of down timber. Despite the thin air, my companions chattered on about a new fly they called the Bloody Butcher, continuing a conversation that had begun at dawn during the drive west from Colorado Springs. I was hardly impressed. Tied with a body of glaring, fluorescent red silk overwrapped by brown hackle, the Bloody Butcher looked as garish as its name sounded. The fly seemed better suited for Crappie or Blue Gill. I said nothing, concentrating instead on getting a badly needed second wind. One fellow had rigged up at the car, and so the instant we reached the barren tundra banks of Ptarmigan, he sent a Butcher whistling far out into the lake behind a bobber fashioned from a piece of broom handle. The crude rig had hardly splashed down before the rod throbbed against a good fish, even as we shed our packs. The prize turned out to be an unusually beautiful Cutthroat, darkly speckled against a background of golden bronze and splashed with scarlet. Our friend's success made fumbling fingers doubly clumsy as we hurried to assemble our own gear, especially when he hooked a fat Rainbow on his next cast. Eventually, everyone was in action, but for my part, the action consisted of casting and reeling. In those days, I carried an array of lures sufficient to set up a tackle shop right there on the bank so I tried something new every few minutes. Disappointingly, the rare strikes I got were damped by the stretchy spinning line and the hooks skidded free. Despite repeated offers, I refused to borrow one of the crimson creations and the day ended with a final score of 37 trout caught on a Butcher to a lonesome Rainbow

I managed to take on a spoon. In retrospect, I'm glad I was so stubborn, for otherwise, the Butcher's mastery over literally dozens of lures, other fly patterns (and even a few last resort salmon eggs) might not have been clear-cut. At the time, none of us knew why the Bloody Butcher had lived up to its name so well. Was this just luck, was the fly really magical or was there a biological explanation? A ratio of 37 to 1 couldn't very well be luck, and I doubted that the trout were interested in magic acts. Actually the way in which my friends fished the Butcher provided a clue, had I known enough to recognize it. The fly worked best when twitched along within a few inches of the surface by starting the retrieve immediately after a cast, taking a sharp turn or two on the reel, pausing and reeling again. A little research revealed that many high lakes support huge populations of fresh water shrimp. Certain of these Crustacea have yellowish to reddish-orange shells and are highly prized by trout, as reflected by the pink color of their flesh. In retrospect, I remembered seeing remnants of shrimp in the bellies of a few fish we stored in a snowbank for dinner, as well as the striking color of their tissues when they were cleaned. Thus the Butcher's gaudy hue, size and shape, coupled with a quick jumpy swimming retrieve, added up to a

BLOODY BUTCHER

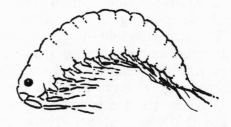

SHRIMP

very deadly presentation. Incidentally, the trout were taking within easy fly-rod range on Ptarmigan, and it would have been interesting to match a Butcher fished on a fly rod against one presented by means of spinning gear.

On today's crowded streams, there's justifiable concern over the population explosion among anglers. However, I would submit that flies are being neglected on some waters to an extent that trout are no longer used to seeing them! For example, the finny residents of a hard-fished pool might be shown salmon eggs, several popular spoons and spinners, purple plastic worms, real worms, corn, and finally some fluorescent, cheese-flavored marshmallow balls for dessert, all in the same day, and without so much as a glimpse of an artificial fly. Lest this seem farfetched, I recently counted 22 consecutive anglers fishing with bait or lures along the pretty Pecos River headwaters in the Sangre de Cristo Mountains of New Mexico, but I didn't meet one fly fisher. I was surprised that their luck was generally poor, and not a few were fishless, for flies were so productive that a rather ordinary angler could have taken a half dozen trout in an hour, and not just in the heavily stocked areas around campgrounds. Indeed, one of my sons, not yet in his teens, took a number of fish (to the noticeable annoyance of several adults whom we met). It was as if the trout weren't familiar with our artificial flies and found them intriguing. Of course, this sort of emphasis on bait and spinning lures doesn't exist on "fly-only" water, but why confine your fishing to select areas? Sometimes, so many anglers congregate on "quality water" that fishing is better elsewhere, and for that matter, I rather enjoy competing against the spinning clan anyhow!

I've always thought that a psychologist could make an interesting study of fly fishers. I suspect that fly fishing is an ego thing that has its roots in the concept of "conning" the trout. Successfully copying an insect that's natural to the trout's diet is a bit like passing a bogus bill. The knowledge that the victim is superbly equipped to detect such fraud adds to the satisfaction, and fly tiers get an added kick out of doing their own counterfeiting. It's gratifying to find that a little familiarity with food forms that are important to trout can explain why a particular fly or method of presentation is best at one time or another. This gives an angler a handle on why things happen as they do, and ideas about how he may improve his luck through manipulations of tactics and tackle. Potentially, there is a great deal to learn and more to think about than wondering if your worm has disintegrated on the hook.

Fly fishing may be a congenial or a solitary contemplative pastime with as much nature appreciation thrown in as one wishes. The sport is most certainly appealing from an ecological point of view, since it can be, and should be, relatively nondestructive. Delicate fly hooks are usually removable without serious damage in contrast to treble-hooked spinning lures and deeply swallowed bait hooks. I honestly believe that, as a group, fly fishers return a larger proportion of their catch to the water than do their spinning brethren. Some of the latter are "meat men" in the sense that they seem to judge the success of a trip largely on the basis of the size of their bulging creels, whereas fly fishermen tend to be equally interested in the hows, whys, and wheres of their angling. After all, isn't the real challenge a matter of getting the trout landed? The angler has his victory then, and really, there isn't a whole lot of glamour or glory in a dead fish anyway. As to the high cost of food, my wife has been kind enough to do some unsolicited cost accounting of my fishing efforts. According to her possibly biased calculations, pound for pound, trout are much more expensive than lobster!

Outsiders sometimes get the idea that fly fishing is such a fancy diversion that it's more an affectation than a sport. A professor of English (whose hobbies were not of an outdoor sort) once made a rather scathing comment along these lines. It went something like this: "The usual fly fisherman appears to be a foppish fellow, so entangled in the branches of a forest of esthetics that he has lost sight of what he's about." As I interpret this baroque sentence, it suggests that while nonfly fishers may have feet of clay, they at least keep them on the ground, and set out to accomplish what fishermen historically are supposed to accomplish, that is, they try to catch fish. However, as we have seen, this argument has a very large hole in it. From a biological standpoint, it is the fly fisher who holds the high cards, if only he knows how to play them.

I think all this is summarized best by the fact that I have yet to meet a competent fly fisher who prefers another method; by the same token, there is no fly fisherman so zealous as the converted spin-fisher. Are there not parallels in religion?

READING THE WATER

An experienced angler wastes little time on the stream in comparison with a beginner. For one thing, the veteran spends less of the day climbing trees in search of his fly, but there is a much more important aspect. Seasoned fishermen learn to concentrate their time and efforts on those portions of the stream where they will do the most good, and they won't fool with water that isn't likely to produce. This is an acquired skill that has been called "reading the water," a catchy phrase, perhaps, but an accurately descriptive one. Water reading amounts to a visual interpretation of a four dimensional picture in which the fourth dimension, or time, is represented by current. A skilled reader sees all sorts of things which have importance to him that would have no significance whatever for the novice. In final analysis, water reading is really a mapping process wherein the stream is broken up into various areas, zones, or literally, "pieces of water." Each of these pieces has relative value in terms of the likelihood that it will be productive if fished properly, such that one particular area might be a good bet for a strike, while it would be better to ignore zones of fallow water lying immediately adjacent. Nor is this just a matter of identifying big green pools; small children can do that. Large pools are made up of numerous integral parts, like the pieces in a picture puzzle, and these, too, need to be sorted out in the interests of productive angling. For that matter, water reading goes far beyond obvious detail and gets down to recognition of wash-basin sized pockets of water hidden in fast currents.

Water depth and current speed are major features of note for the reader, as is surface texture (slick, finely riffled, choppy, etc.). Add to these the various structural details one sees along the banks and on the bottom, and the overall picture becomes pretty complex. An angler's eyes and mind actually function very much like a computer insofar as sorting out these many observations. The computer readout becomes an action plan — but lest this sound too scientific, I can assure the beginner that an angler doesn't need a Ph.D. in order to read water. I've watched many a youngster pick up the skill almost instinctively, sometimes more quickly than certain adults with whom I've fished who do happen to have advanced degrees!

Water reading is learned on the water, but it's helpful to have some sort of scheme or mental framework as a scaffolding upon which actual experiences can be arranged to hasten the process. My approach is based on the idea that trout evaluate water in a selective manner, too. Admittedly, fish behavior is a matter of instinct rather than thought, but nonetheless, trout act as if they look for three particular qualities within their environment. The first is *cover* or a place to hide from danger, potential or real. Self-preservation is the most primal of instincts, and the amount of cover that a given piece of water provides can vary greatly. I call the second quality *holding*, meaning relative freedom from current. Trout are not immune to the current's pull just because of their streamlined shape and slippery skins. They must expend energy in order to hold their position in a current, or be washed downstream. Obviously, holding quality is also highly variable from one area to another. *Food* content is the third feature, an important one in water reading, because certain portions of a stream may be much richer than others.

Of the three (cover, holding, and food), which is most important? If there were a straightforward answer, water reading would be greatly simplified, but the facts are that the relative values of each shift sharply according to prevailing conditions. Still, there are two general and highly dependable rules that will stand an angler in good stead:

First, the law of supply and demand applies rather neatly to cover, holding, and food; the harder each is to find, the more valued by the trout (a not un-human attitude).

Second, trout will venture into areas that are poor in cover or holding for only one reason, and that is food, again a very natural reaction.

The final "worth" of a certain piece of water is the sum of its values for cover, holding, and food, whatever their individual importance may be. Certain areas are going to rate low right across the board and should be thought of as "waste water." Others will grade uniformly high, deserving a premium label, but between these extremes, there are all manner of intermediate value pieces about which the fisherman will have to make some sort of decision.

Holding is the easiest quality to visualize, for current speed is plainly evident. Cover is less obvious. Cover is not just a matter of the availability of places for trout to hide, such as weed beds or undercut banks. There are three additional factors: water clarity, depth, and surface texture. Trout seem more secure when there is a degree of murkiness and the same is true when they are in deep water, regardless of clarity. An irregular wavy surface is difficult for the angler to see through, and probably for trout as well. Interestingly, fish react to this kind of surface as if it provided them with a sort of security blanket. In a deep quiet pool, cover and holding ratings are complementary, but in other situations they may tend to cancel one another, as in a boiling current.

There are several stream features that correlate directly with food content. Currents get a high grade in this respect by compressing relatively large volumes of water into a small area. Currents are very much like funnels in that they drain a broader region above them, just as a funnel's mouth is larger than its spout. Since food is carried in and on the water, a current truly concentrates it for the trout, and hence for the fisherman, too. Currents come in all sizes from huge chutes draining virtually an entire river's flow down to minor tongues scattered all over the surface of a swift stream, but whatever its width and strength, a current still accumulates food to some extent. Of course current and holding are mutually exclusive, and so this is another example of the need to deal with pieces of water having mixed values. A second basic food fact is that another potentially important portion of a stream's supply comes from its banks. An overhanging grassy or willow strewn bank, as in a meadow, may play the role of a virtual cornucopia by spilling a profusion of grasshoppers, caterpillars, beetles, ants, etc. into the water where trout await in eager anticipation. I suppose that these are accidents of nature in which terrestrial or land-dwelling insects meet a watery end; however, the trout don't worry about the whys and wherefores of their diet, and neither should we. It follows that water along lush, undercut banks should theoretically pick up food value (not to mention potential cover and holding). Flat rocky banks have less to offer in this regard.

One of the fundamental principles in water reading involves an analogy to the real estate business, wherein pieces of property sometimes derive much of their value because of proximity to other more desirable areas with commercial, residential, or recreational potential. Similarly, a piece of water with only fair intrinsic value may borrow from its surroundings. Take a strong current with sharply defined margins. The water inches away from the edge of the flow is going to rate much higher for holding than the water within current, yet is within easy reach of a virtual pipeline of food. Trout will dart into such currents momentarily, capture an insect and return to their nearby holding positions. It is noteworthy that the edges of a swift current commonly produce better than the very center, and that there is an additionally important if narrow strip of water just to either side of these current edges. Another practical instance of value borrowing is seen in cover-poor shallows as they approach a grassy bank. Now and then, a trout's choice of water will surprise you when food is at stake. I recall a particularly fine Brown that I took from the Encampment River in Wyoming as the result of a poor cast at a time when I really wasn't trying to catch anything, strange as that may seem. It was a hot afternoon; the trout were apparently napping, and so I stopped fishing in order to test an experimental leader designed for casting small flies. Ahead lay a long stretch of slow shallows backing up to an overhanging grassy bank on my left. The good part of the river was along the opposite bank in the form of a deep channel, but I wanted to see how the new leader would perform in the face of a breeze, and so, fixing my sights on a smooth rock just above water level about 40 feet upstream, I began practice casting a tiny fly onto its surface. I was getting the feel of the new leader when a slight shift in the wind sent my next cast off target some 12 feet to the left and onto the grassy overhang. Irritated, I twitched the fly free, but before I could pick it up for another cast, an enormous trout slurped it down literally within inches of the water edge. I was too dumbfounded to set the hook; he had to do it for me. Later, when I waded back to inspect the spot from which my trophy had attacked, the water averaged only 10 inches in depth. He had burst from a hidden pocket under the bank, perhaps a little deeper and canopied by long blades of grass. I could only conclude that this crafty fellow had been willing to trade really safe cover for a close shot at land-dwelling appetizers (grasshoppers, I suspect), meanwhile enjoying comfortable holding. Incidentally, this is a lazy life style that Browns especially enjoy. This incident sticks in my memory, for try as I might, I couldn't catch another fish approaching this one. It's a bit humbling when your best results are based on sheer luck!

Currents and banks notwithstanding, food content is the hardest of the three qualities to read. This is because the activities of the aquatic insects upon which trout feed are both transient and variable as to the kind of water in which they take place. Insects have a way of becoming available

in one or another type of water where there were few or none before, and for as long as they persist, they confer tremendous food value on that area, whether in a current or otherwise. The renowned May flies in particular are capable of creating sudden bursts of extreme feeding excitement when they hatch from immature nymph forms into young adult flies called "duns." This takes place over fairly short periods of time and in water of a type peculiar to the species of May fly that's involved. In the process of struggling to shed the final nymphal skin in the surface film, the May fly is in an awkward and precarious position, becoming easy prey for the trout. Certain species hatch in currents, others from slow water — some in shallows, and others from the depths. The nature of the bottom is critical too; sand, silt, rocks, or beds of moss — each has its own population of nymph species, and as such, each is a distinctive launching pad for different hatches. Wherever the event occurs, food values skyrocket until, in Cinderella fashion, the hatch comes to an end, sometimes as abruptly as if a clock had indeed chimed the hour!

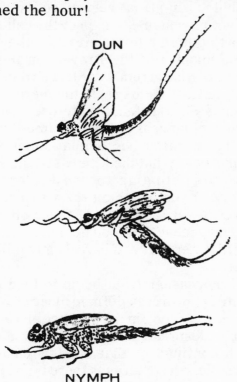

DUN

NYMPH

Hatch/rise activity may be clearly evident and even dramatic on the one hand, or so subtle that it's difficult to spot either the antics of the insects or the corresponding feeding response of the trout. I very nearly missed some remarkable dry-fly action on this account while fishing the Big Laramie River near the Colorado-Wyoming border. The morning was off to a promising start with several brief May fly hatches, when a front moved down the valley just after noon, accompanied by a nasty rain squall and refrigerated by snowbanks capping the high Rawah Peaks to the south. This storm seemed to bring fishing for the day to a premature end; after a sterile afternoon, I was seriously considering an early dinner when clouds broke to the west, and the sun reappeared at about 5:00 p.m. I found myself at the lower end of a favorite segment of river channel, and so in hopes of seeing a rise, I began to work my way slowly upstream,

absently flipping a fly into the main current. Soon, peculiar flashes of light just over the water caught the corner of my eye from far above. Here, the streambed pitched steeply such that the whole river pounded and churned over a rocky washboard into slow water below. I paid little attention at first, assuming that these were mirror-like reflections from leaping wavelets and plumes of spray, but the glints continued and not always in the same spot. Curious, I stopped casting and moved up for a closer look. My intention was to continue back to the ranch, but that plan evaporated instantly when I found a prodigious rise in progress. Indeed, as many as a half-dozen trout were airborne at any one time above the racing water. It was their shiny flanks, acting as reflectors, that had attracted my attention! Close inspection revealed a hatch of grey May fly duns coming off the surging surface, and surprisingly, both the hatch and the rise were virtually confined to the current chute. Although a few fish dimpled where the rapids spilled into quiet water just below, the river above the chute was dead for as far as I could see. The anxious risers literally swallowed any reasonable imitation with reckless abandon, and it was no trick to release 14 fat Browns in an hour of hectic action. The chute provided good cover, thanks to its boiling surface, although holding quality was almost nil, and I was sure that most of the ferocious feeders had moved into the area from adjacent waters. Frankly, I would have ordinarily walked around this stretch without more than a glance had not the slanting rays of the sun given me a valuable assist in water reading. When the hatch began to dwindle, I moved quickly upstream to another rapids, noting an absence of surface rises in the quiet water I passed. Sure enough, duns of the same species were coming off this swift current too, much to the excitement of the Browns who frequented that neighborhood. Thus, on this particular afternoon, for a period of about 90 minutes, the nymphs of a certain May fly chose to become duns — and in so doing, created enormous food value in a kind of water

9

natural to that species.

There is a tendency for one or another kind of insect (especially May flies) to hatch at about the same time each day over a span of consecutive days for as long as several weeks. I naturally anticipated a repeat performance by the Big Laramie duns, but a cloudburst the next morning changed the plans of their nymphs, for they declined to perform in the high muddy water that followed, and we had to leave the next day.

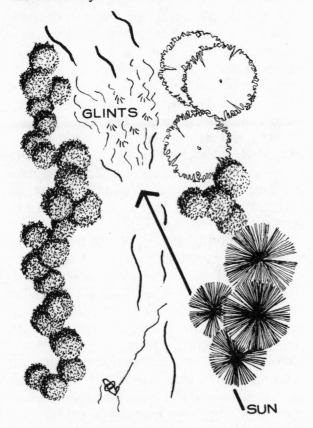

GLINTS

SUN

A hatch often apppears first at some point relatively low along a river's course, gradually moving upstream with time. The emergence of huge Stone or Willow flies, so well known to western anglers before many famous rivers fell prey to the dam builders, actually moved up river day by day, covering miles at a time. The hatch may be triggered by warming water, although in spring-fed streams, temperature is almost constant, and other mechanisms such as the average duration of daylight may play a role in setting the so-called biological clock for the trout. These exciting events can occur at any time from early morning until dark; however, hatches of specific insects tend to begin at about the same time each day, a fact of obvious interest for fishermen.

As we have seen, turbulent surfaces can hide rising trout very effectively, and it is not reasonable to expect the fish to go cavorting high into the air when they rise in the manner of the Browns on the Big Laramie. Rises from very large trout may be so delicate as to create the merest dimple on a slick surface; therefore, continuing surveillance is a must. At times the tip-off that a hatch has begun comes from finding newly hatched duns struggling in the water, clinging to brush along the banks or from watching the airspace just above the surface. Any of these observations may mean that food has become available in water that was barren only minutes before.

On occasion, trout begin to feed in an isolated pool or less-defined piece of water, such as a current, in the absence of a general or widespread rise. Sometimes, a local hatch confined to that small area is responsible, but sometimes there is no identifiable explanation. When a group spreads out to work a stream at the same time, one angler may run into a bonanza area like this while everyone else is having a tough time of it. Whatever the cause, these events are real enough, and add to the luck factor in fishing. This is one of many reasons why stream fishing should be an action sport. When things are slow, it's a very good plan to stay alert and keep moving; a hot spot may await just around the next bend!

Big pools remind me of golf courses in a way, because they have so many component parts that can be fished separately, just as holes are played one at a time. However, an angler has the option of choosing the order in which he wishes to fish the pieces and can vary the amount of attention each receives. It may take an hour or more to "play a pool" carefully. I suppose you could even keep score by adding up the total number of strikes or hooked fish from each part of the pool. I would have preferred to use a photograph of a pool to illustrate these points, but unfortunately, photographs do a very poor job of depicting depth and also current, that vital fourth dimension in water reading. Instead, I have defined briefly a group of common terms for easily recognizable types of water, each with a simple diagrammatic symbol, for we can then use these word-diagram building blocks to assemble a typical pool. (Shading correlates with depth, and arrows show current direction; the heavier the line, the stronger the current.)

Channel Current:

A strong, reasonably deep current that carries a good part of the stream's flow. Poor holding is combined with good food and cover potential.

Channel Current:

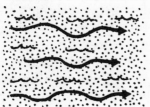

Glide:

Another current, but this time of medium or slow speed and featuring a slick surface. Glides often form at the tail of a channel current.

Glide:

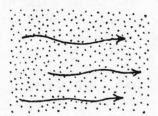

Riffle:

Shallow, fairly rapid water flowing over a flat bottom and covered by a system of close-spaced, tiny wavelets. This is the preferred water for the larvae of certain insects.

Riffle:

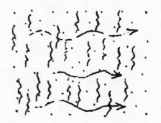

Feeding Current:

Feeding Current:
(Feeding Riffle)

A very special kind of water that may form the tail of a channel, develop as a broad band along the edge of a swift current or arise in the crotch between merging currents. The characteristically choppy surface is marked by small waves, more slowly moving and less regular than those in a riffle. Of moderate depth, feeding currents appear quite strong, as if they would be tough to wade. However, the water actually tumbles and churns along in a peculiar way, lacking a firm thrust, yet still collecting lots of food.

(Feeding Riffle)

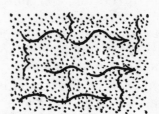

Eddy:
An area of relatively deep water just to one side of a strong current. Eddies are created by a finger of flow that curls back from the main current, scooping out the bottom. This backflow causes eddy water to stir about in slow whirlpool fashion, meanwhile capturing food from the channel. Eddies have a lot going for them!

Eddy:

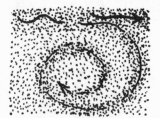

Our classical demonstration pool decorates an otherwise rapid segment of Colorado's White River, a good-sized stream that arises among spectacular mountain plateaus in the northwestern part of the state. About 50 feet in width, this pool owed its existence to a flat rock bar that jutted suddenly into the channel from the left bank (facing upstream). Acting as a dike, the bar collected, diverted, and channeled much of the river's flow toward the sheer cliffs along the right bank. The stream above the pool was wide and shoal for fully a half mile, and as the boiling current chute skidded around the tip of the dike, it drained a large area, very much like the tapering spout of a funnel.

I customarily worked this pool in an upstream direction, beginning with the riffle. Only a foot or so in depth, cover was still fair, thanks to a dancing surface, and the water bounced along lightly, so holding was also reasonable. Food values fluctuated greatly. Infrequently, a hatch of May flies created an obvious rise, or nymphs destined to become adults at some later date would leave the safety of coarse gravel in which they had burrowed to swim or crawl about. Either event attracted

hordes of eager trout, although much of the time the riffle was quiet. I made it a habit to test this area for at least a few minutes with sunken flies in the event of hidden, sub-surface feeding activity.

Along the cliff face ran a distinctive, slick-surfaced glide. Even where the stream was as much as three feet deep, the smallest details on the smooth rocky bottom were evident through the clear water, and so cover was sketchy. Born of the channel current, the glide had lost a great deal of its velocity so that trout sometimes hung motionless, finning slowly, while awaiting food coming down the chute from above. Unless I could see trout in the glide, it seldom produced, and therefore a close visual check determined whether it was worth working.

The channel current rated zero for holding, of course, although its depth and rough surface meant fine cover. The channel offered a better supply of food than did the glide, for it compressed far more of the river's flow before fanning out to fill the broad riffle and glide. This channel was the real funnel spout and, as such, always received a thorough probing.

Along the entire left side of the pool lay a large strip of shallow water with few redeeming features. The cobblestone bottom provided little cover, and the flat rocky bank added almost no food value; there was plenty of holding water in adjacent areas anyway. I soon learned that it was a waste of time to fish the shallow slack.

The deep slack zone almost seemed out of place, as if it were a tiny pond stuck into the midst of an otherwise fast-moving pool system. Cover and holding were of the highest quality, but food content must have been meagre, for I sometimes spent 15 minutes watching a floating fly bob along, unmolested on its still surface, or I could slowly trawl a sunken fly through its depths without reward. This area ordinarily deserved no more than a lick and a promise.

The eddy was like money in the bank. In fact, I can't recall fishing it without getting a couple of strikes, and yet its cover and holding characteristics were much like those in the deep slack. The difference

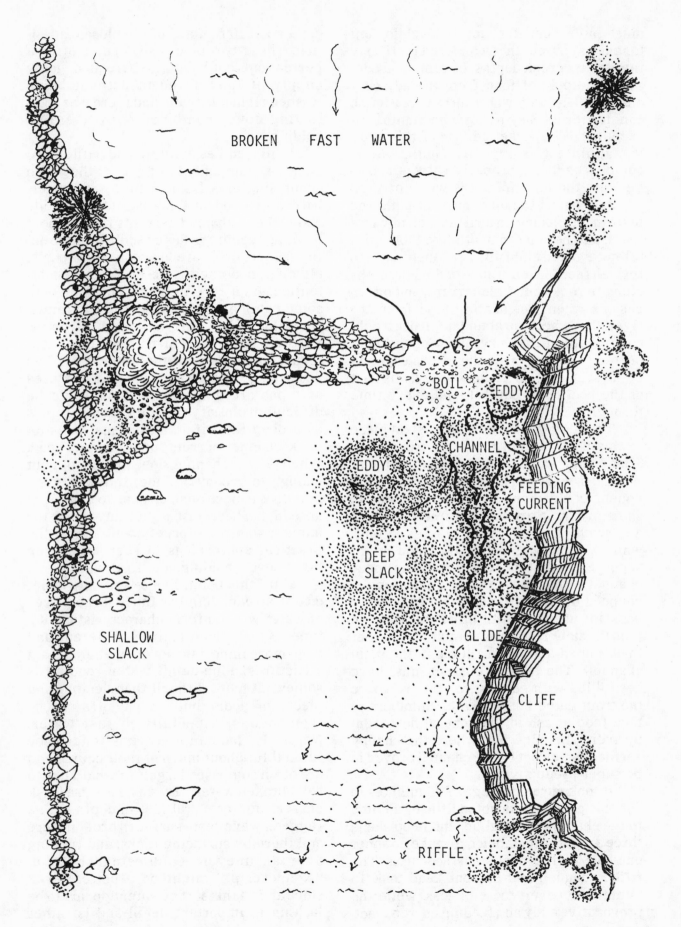

BROKEN FAST WATER

BOIL

EDDY

CHANNEL

EDDY

FEEDING CURRENT

DEEP SLACK

SHALLOW SLACK

GLIDE

CLIFF

RIFFLE

must have been the gently backflowing tongue of current that wandered restlessly through its green depths, filtering in a continuing supply of food from the adjacent channel. The eddy was a sort of free lunch counter for its easy-living inhabitants. (An excellent vest pocket edition of this eddy lay against the opposite bank, but it couldn't be fished properly without crossing, and the next ford was well upriver.)

Just below the dike, current gathered to form the channel in a virtual boil of white foam, and here large, moth-like Stone flies often cavorted clumsily, perilously close to the surface. Their thick-bodied nymphs clung to rocks amid the torrent, and on occasions when free-floating food from the river above became abundant, trout would congregate in the very midst of the boil, perfectly hidden, as if they were eager to be "first at table." Needless to say, this part of the pool got a careful trial every time through.

The eddy was the most consistent piece of this pool, but not the most productive. That honor went to the feeding current. When fish were working actively, this component could yield a half-dozen trout in short order. It was about three feet deep and wave tossed; cover was excellent, while holding was better than one might suppose. A splinter of current off the upper channel swung away at a fairly sharp angle, bounced off the cliff face, and ricocheted back to interfere with other currents so that the flow front was tumultuous rather than unified and powerful (as in the main channel). The feeding current must have been filled with edibles, for this is where the trout gathered in greatest numbers to take food awash in the general flow from upriver. The edge just where the choppy surface was swept by the channel proved to be super-productive.

It took me an average of 40 minutes to fish this pool, yet I devoted little or no time to the shallow slack, glide, and deep slack, three areas that combined to make up about one-half of the pool's surface area. The riffle, channel, and current head took 15 minutes to cover, more or less, while the provocative eddy and feeding current each got a good 10 minutes of my closest attention. These two pieces seemed to offer a perfect current balance where an ongoing supply of food sifted in without being washed right out again, and there was comforting cover combined with tolerable holding.

While eddies, glides, and riffles are common components of pools, they also occur singly as isolated pieces of water. Riffles develop in the absence of a glide above them, channel currents fade without forming feeding riffles or eddies, and so on. In essence, these are loose pieces of pools, although nonetheless deserving of our attention. As a case in point, take the lonesome patch of rapids on the Big Laramie, teeming with mirror-sided Browns. Further, many parts of a stream don't conform neatly to any of the water types I've described, because hybrids and mixtures of types are commonplace. It would be difficult to classify the Big Laramie rapids as a deep fast riffle, an unusual bank-to-bank channel current, or a current head. When does a channel slow and smooth out enough to become a glide, and how much flow does a piece of slack need to qualify as an eddy? There just aren't any rules for naming water, so forget about terms, the practical approach is to keep an eye on basic cover, holding, and food values.

Until this point, I've talked only about coarse stream detail or fairly large pieces of water with uniform characteristics. It's time to look at an entirely different and even more important set of smaller stream structures. Fine-detail water reading is somewhat more difficult than deciphering pieces of pools, but the pay-offs can be tremendous, especially in fast water. Naturally, mountain streams tend to be rapid throughout much of their course and are often composed largely of what I like to call "broken water." By this, I mean a brisk current up to several feet in depth with a ragged, wave-torn surface, broken here and there by surfacing rocks, and running over an uneven, cobblestone bottom. "Nondescript" might be a better term, since at first this sort of water appears to be lacking in important detail and is rather monotonous. Nothing could be further from the truth. Those who know how to read broken water see a fascinating complex of small features, and more to the point, they translate what they read into amazing catches. There are two excellent, common sense reasons for learning to read and to fish broken water. First, it frequently produces better than the pretty, deep, green pools. I have seen this over and over each season in streams of all size so this isn't a now-and-then phenomenon. Beware the not unnatural assumption that deep, slow water of pool type is the best a stream has to offer! Secondly, as I have indicated, much of your competition is likely to come from the spinning clan, armed with their bait and lures. It's a fact that few of them can read broken water, and consequently few attempt to fish it. These are strictly "pool people." Let's assume that 80 percent of a certain stream's surface is broken water and 20 percent is found in pools. If four of five fishermen are of the spinning variety, as is likely, at least 80 percent of the pressure will be concentrated on only 20 percent of the water. This is not so much of an exaggeration as it may seem, admitting that there are skillful spin fishers who work broken water, just as there are fly fishermen who remain glued to the pools. I like to think that the big pools take a great deal of pressure off the rest of the stream, and I suggest that it makes good sense to beat the system. I like people, but I'd prefer to rub elbows back in the city rather than around the banks of some deep pool. When you stop to consider, the pool people see and fish an entirely different stream than those of us who can deal with the nondescript flat water!

So how to proceed? There is a small and very common piece of water called a "rock pocket" that provides an ideal introduction to broken-water reading. These are actually tiny pools that form below a surfacing rock where tongues of accelerating current sweep around either side of the deflector, leaving a smooth eddy just behind the rock. The twin currents eventually merge, and the pool is "over," but it's easy to see

that these pockets provide holding, cover, and also small food-concentrating currents. With the concept of a rock pocket in mind, imagine now that the rock is totally submerged. Will the same holding-cover-food features still obtain? Absolutely. Good holding is not the exclusive property of quiet pools or zones of slack, nor is cover dependent on depth, a riffled surface, undercut banks, and the like. Current deflectors such as small clumps of water weed, drowned branches, and rocks no larger than your hat create perfectly acceptable "windows" of holding water in the swiftest current, as well as pockets of cover. Banks also present fine-detail pockets, due to irregularities in contour, protruding roots, and boulders. It's important to realize that a trout or a cluster of several fish doesn't need or demand very large holding windows or cover nooks. Indeed, the downstream side of a basketball-diameter rock sticking up a bit above the bottom may be home to several sizable trout.

ROCK POCKET

It took me longer to learn broken-water reading than I like to admit. My training ground was Colorado's White River, mentioned in conjunction with the pool diagram. The White's South Fork is almost a pure culture of fast, foam-flecked currents,

15

interrupted now and then by a big pool. As a youngster, I fished these pools exclusively during our annual pack trip. The rest of the river was a total mystery to me, and it was comforting to know that the pools at least *contained* trout, whether I could catch them or not. My days were planned very much in the manner of a postman's route, in that regular stops were made at each pool in sequence, leading away from and back to camp. I actually trotted along the banks between holes, dodging clumps of sagebrush and getting plenty of exercise while wasting a lot of potential fishing time. Gradually, I began to recognize small replicas of the large pools, doll-house copies fed by smaller currents and not nearly so deep as those you could swim in. I was gratified to find that these mini-pools yielded more trout per fishing hour than did the big green pools, and I cut down on my jogging activities somewhat, although there were still long stretches of barren water. At least, I assumed they were barren until one evening when I found myself trapped in the middle of a half-mile stretch of flat, broken water between two groups of fishermen. There was insufficient time to walk around them before dark, and so it was a matter of either quitting or tackling the unreadable water. Everything about the river in my area was the same; depth, current, surface texture, and the cobblestone bottom all blended into one dull, characterless picture. Having no better plan, I attempted to single out prominent rocks that protruded into the current a bit more than their neighbors with the idea of swimming my wet fly past them. The results were shocking. Now "shocking" is almost always an exaggeration — however, in this case, I was honestly shocked, for an eager Rainbow or Cutthroat grabbed the fly almost every time it swept by one of these tiny targets. It seemed impossible that so many fish would choose to live in such poor water. Could it be that my idea of poor water was not the same as theirs? A whole new world unfolded over the next few days as I began to see wash-basin-sized pockets all over the river, and more to the point, they produced in rabbit-

from-the-hat fashion to an extent that my daily catches doubled. You might think that broken-water trout would run small, but these fish actually averaged two inches longer than those taken from my favorite pools, and they were fatter and more feisty, as if their rigorous environment had made them particularly fit. I quickly became addicted to the fast broken water, so much so that I found myself preferentially walking around the pools! Reading this kind of water is neither a natural talent nor an easily acquired skill. It takes time to learn, but the rewards are worth whatever it takes. For the serious fly fisherman, this kind of reading capacity isn't an option, it's an essential!

Shallow, swift water may be difficult to interpret when features are fine, but so is deep, slow water where details are coarse and yet subtle. Take a wide, serpentine river such as the Green in Wyoming. Its lush, willow-clogged banks are home to the ungainly moose and to all manner of wildlife, including repellent-loving mosquitos of near sparrow caliber. The Green River is literally a natural zoo, or as someone once called it, "the Nile of the Rockies." Although the river is a picture trout stream against the backdrop of the high Wind River Range, reading it is tough. The water looks the same from bend to bend as far as the eye can see, as if it were a skinny, drawn-out lake. It takes time to realize that although depth, current, bottom, and surface detail are quite uniform, minor features still point out channel currents, feeding currents, and eddies, etc. You've just got to get used to waters like the Green and live with them for awhile.

For me, a great deal of the interest in water reading is tied into changes brought about by weather and the seasons. Since angling tactics are based on reading, this is a practical sort of interest. Early season and post-storm conditions feature high, often discolored water. Banks get partially submerged, currents quicken, and the whole picture takes on added detail. Cover should be plentiful, but holding water becomes scarce, and under extreme conditions, productive water reading boils down to finding the holding areas, almost to the exclusion of other features. Late season brings a "mirror image" when streams are shrunken and clear. Banks are high and dry, and currents have lost their punch so that the cover-holding relationship is reversed. It's an excellent plan to simply fish the cover, because trout won't venture far from safety unless an unusually tempting food source comes along. May's methods won't do for July, nor will midsummer's tactics earn a passing grade without appropriate modifications in the fall.

No two streams read exactly alike, and this is probably a good thing. The same story gets old after awhile, but nonetheless, all streams share certain features, and some are remarkably similar. In this regard, I remember my first visit to the headwaters of the Boise River in central Idaho. As we set up our tackle, I had an odd feeling that I had fished this water before, I felt strangely at home. Over the next half-hour, it dawned on me that this stream was a near perfect replica of Colorado's White River, right down to the brush and conifers along the bank. Almost automatically, I switched from a dry fly to a nymph pattern that had been effective on the other river. Somehow I wasn't surprised to find that it was still deadly when fished in the "accustomed places" and in the old ways. It was an uncanny realization that water reading learned 25 years before and a thousand miles away was still perfectly valid. Similarities notwithstanding, the more waters an angler learns, the more educated he becomes, and the better able to cope with new situations.

This chapter cannot hope or pretend to show a new fisherman how to proceed in any detail. The idea was to provide some basis for thoughtful observation along the stream. In final analysis, water reading amounts to mentally photographing your fly in relationship to its surroundings whenever something *good* happens — that is, a hooked fish, or maybe just a tentative rise. Included are depth, current, surface, kind of bottom, and so on. The idea is to stock a memory bank with information of a positive nature. The mind has a remarkable capacity to computerize even forgotten and subconscious detail. Eventually an angler begins to pick productive targets instinctively, and like the trout, performs without really thinking. First however, he has to stock his stream computer with the right data, because words are no substitute for actual experiences.

FIGURING THE FLOAT

Is it better to fish upstream or down? This is among the most common queries raised at seminars, and while the question is simple enough, the answers are not. In the first place, the real importance of upstream versus downstream has to be translated into a decision between two basic ways of presenting a fly. One is ideally suited for casting against the current, or upstream, and the other for fishing with the current in a downstream direction. The way in which the fly is presented when the trout see it in or on the water frequently governs their response, in fact so much so that fly behavior can mean the difference between a fine catch and a thorough skunking.

The upstream presentation is called "natural drift" or "dead drift"; I use the terms interchangeably. Here the fly floats along passively wherever the current chooses to take it, as if there were no leader and line attached. The idea is to suggest an insect that isn't swimming on its own, floating either on the surface or beneath it.

"Drag retrieve," the alternative downstream method, involves activation of the fly. There is no way to push a fly on the end of a flexible line and leader, so it has to be pulled through the water. Thus the fly is made to swim on its own and is given apparent life.

As noted, upstream fishermen depend heavily on the natural or dead drift, while members of the downstream fraternity are devoted to drag retrieves, but before attacking the pros and cons of natural drifts and drag presentations, let's look at why this is so.

When an angler who is fishing natural drift casts upstream, the current obligingly carries his fly into and through the target water and eventually back to him in the manner of a dog retrieving a stick. Meanwhile, the angler's free hand pulls in accumulating slack line so that there is little left for the rod to pick up, and the next cast

is easily launched. In contrast, natural drifting downstream amounts to letting the fly out into the current on a tether (the line and leader). This is a tricky proposition, because it's necessary to feed out line just faster than the current pulls it away. Otherwise the line will come taut, interfering with the fly's natural float. No matter how slight, this impedence results in *drag,* and drag defeats the whole purpose behind natural drifting, at least the trout usually seem to think so. Oddly enough, fish that are taking a true dead drift with enthusiasm will frequently turn tail at the sight of the very same fly presented with a bit of drag, even if the impedence is barely perceptible! Thus, for the most part, natural drifting is an "all or none" presentation, and drag is to be avoided at all costs. Apart from the need for deft release of line, downstream dead drifts are cumbersome and tedious because the further the fly floats, the more line there is to retrieve before making the next presentation. Of course, the line can be reeled back in, but this takes time, and it is neither easy nor practical to lift a long line from the water by means of a backcast. Pulling a floating fly back after a long downstream float is quite likely to submerge and soak it so that the fly has to be dried before it will float again. It may seem foolish to place so much emphasis on whether the current helps or hinders in line retrieval, but over the course of several fishing hours, the difference becomes plenty obvious. It's infinitely more simple to let the current work *for* you!

Aside from an occasional flutter, insects floating on the surface are fairly immobile. It follows that dry flies are traditionally fished dead drift, and hence upstream.

Drag retrieves are perfect for downstream fishing with sunken flies, for the current often partially eliminates casting chores by carrying the fly to its target. However, this doesn't mean that wets should always be fished downstream. Indeed, the wet-fly fisherman has a vitally important "up-down" decision to make, or more exactly, a choice between natural drifts and drag retrieves. Downstream drag retrieving is certainly the easier and less demanding method. Wading down with the current pushing from behind is not nearly so tiring as fighting against it. Further, when a trout hits the fly, his strike will be virtually telegraphed up the line, down the rod, and to your hand, perhaps only as a gentle tug, but there is still a signal to set the hook. Dead drifting a sunken fly upstream, on the other hand, creates a rather perplexing problem. In contrast to a visible, floating fly bobbing along on top, the angler will often be unable to follow a wet fly due to its depth, murky water, or surface glare, and so he has to fish "blind." But worse, the line needs to be somewhat slack, or the fly will drag, and yet just a tiny bit of slack is going to damp out the force of a strike, should a fish happen to take. Now this is a psychologically devastating state of affairs, for if the strike is neither seen nor felt, how is the angler to know when his fly is being attacked in time to jerk back and set the hook?

There's just no question — downstream drag retrieving is the simplest way to present a wet fly, but as in so many endeavors, the easy way is not necessarily the best way! In the first place, it would appear that a great deal of the food trout take from beneath the surface comes to them drifting naturally. No one knows this better than skillful bait and lure fishermen, for many of them also work upstream. I'm really not sure that there is a prevalence of free-floating food over the swimming variety; however, I am sure that the natural drift is the most *consistently* productive method of presentation, regardless of locale or time of season. It is the traditional and orthodox presentation, if you will. But how to get that invisible hook home? It's not an impossible feat at all, thanks to a technique we can call slack-line striking. This is a matter of watching the line end or leader for changes in the direction or speed of float caused by the strike. Although slack-line striking requires some experience and concentration, it's not very difficult, and the technique really works! I've pushed a detailed explanation all the way back to Chapter 15 because I want to introduce several pertinent considerations concerning tactics and tackle first. (The reader may wish to jump ahead and scan this material briefly for a grasp of what slack-line striking is all about.)

The downstream traveling drag retriever also buys into potential trouble based on the fact that trout almost invariably lie facing upstream. This means that he is going to greet them eye to eye, while an upstream fisherman approaches his quarry from the rear. In addition, mud, sand, silt, and other debris kicked up from the bottom during a downstream approach gets carried into the very faces of the fish below, as will surface disturbance rings and water vibrations. None of these warning signs can very well travel upstream unless the current is pretty sluggish.

Nonetheless, one presentation is relatively easy, and the other is more difficult; human nature being as it is, many anglers become addicted to the second-best method. From time to time, I've fallen into this trap too, and it has usually cost me some good fishing. In the early days, I fished Colorado's White River with wet flies during our yearly trek, depending on upstream natural drifts for the most part. One morning, while wading back to the bank, I found myself just above a nice little rock pocket. I was there and the pocket was there, and so, dropping an artificial nymph into the current on one side of the rock, I continued toward the bank, paying more attention to the slippery bottom than to my fly. Suddenly, as the nymph swung back and forth between the twin currents, a smashing strike knocked me off balance, and nearly falling, I found myself fast to a heavy Rainbow. A second rock pocket downriver that caught my eye promptly yielded another fish, and convinced that I had stumbled onto a magical method, I set off in search of similar targets. It happened that this particular area didn't have a great deal of the kind of water I was after, but almost every tiny pool behind a surfacing rock was good for a strike. When I returned to camp that evening, I was surprised to find that everyone else had experienced poor fishing, including several senior anglers more skillful than I. As you might imagine, the next morning found me ready for some fast "rock pocketing" in a rugged, boulder-strewn canyon noted for its heavy trout. Nor was I disappointed; action was terrific. By mid-afternoon, I counted more than 50 strikes, yet only two fish had been hooked — and both of them escaped. I was getting skunked in the midst of plenty! In my frustration, I managed to fall into the river not once but several times, until, thoroughly beaten and angry, I finally gave up. On the long trail back to camp, I gloomily contemplated the dubious joys of hiking in wet Levis together with the fickleness of trout, for it really seemed as if they had been teasing me. As the miles passed, a long-overdue light gradually began to dawn. I had just put in six hours of drag retrieving without once trying a dead drift! By this time, the smell of the campfire filled the air and dusk was at hand; however, a scant half-hour of orthodox presentations with the same nymph produced four good trout, while interspersed drag retrieves continued to bring only strikes. I've since learned that the strikes I felt that day were in reality tentative nips at the rear end of my nymph by curious but highly skeptical trout. Although it's hard to understand these temporary preferences, they are surely real enough. Possibly there were numerous free-swimming nymphs in the rock pockets that first day, accounting for the dragged fly's popularity while free-floating food prevailed on the second. Regardless, I suspect that I largely wasted what might have been a banner day by neglecting the orthodox presentation. During the final three days of the trip, natural drifts continued their superiority, although action was never nearly so fast as on that second day.

It's pretty obvious that I have a strong bias for the natural drift, but it is also noteworthy that in the preceding anecdote there was one day when drag retrieves were clearly more effective. This suggests that it is advisable to test several presentations on a regular basis rather than assuming that one particular method is going to be best.

I have been discussing fishing upstream and down as if the angler *had* to present his fly either against or with the current, parallel to the axis of flow. Of course this is not so. In fact, an angler standing in the center of a sizable stream has 360 degrees worth of casting angles potentially available to him. More practically, we can cut this "casting pie" into eight wedges, one essentially straight up, one straight down, and three to either side. Each of these casting avenues comes in handy from time to time.

There are all sorts of good reasons for fishing at an angle with the current; simple convenience is one. In the process of working a piece of primary target water, smaller or less-important areas of interest commonly present themselves on all sides. If the angler stops to wade over and fish each one as it comes along, upstream or down, he's going to lose time, and if wading is difficult, he can wear himself out in the bargain. It makes sense to work at least some targets lateral to your position via short, cross-stream casts, fishing "sidesaddle," so to speak. Then there are those situations when the water that intrigues you can't be fished in the most desirable way because of fast or deep water or casting obstacles such as brush or overhanging tree limbs. These targets often have to be worked from unusual angles. The pool I diagrammed in the last chapter with a small eddy trapped against a cliff along the righthand bank shows a pretty pocket that was absolutely inaccessible from below or from either side, due to a combination of unwadeable water and the sheer rock wall, so that the only solution was to get at it from above. Like it or not, I had no choice but to lower my fly on a carefully controlled slack line, quartering and downstream, until it found its way into the eddy swirl. (My records show that there was a 60 percent chance of hooking a fish here despite the unaccustomed presentation.) Wind too can force you out of the casting plane you would normally employ for fishing a certain piece of water. By changing your position relative to the target, the wind can sometimes become more of an asset than a liability. Another highly practical consideration has to do with avoidance of surface glare, a real problem in fly visibility. Glare can be severe in the axis of current flow when there is very little from the cross-stream view. Then there is always the danger of spooking trout by allowing the line or butt end of the leader to pass directly over them before the fly makes its appearance, a catastrophe called "lining." These are not exactly the most subtle portions of the tackle chain, and displaying them does little to enhance one's chances.

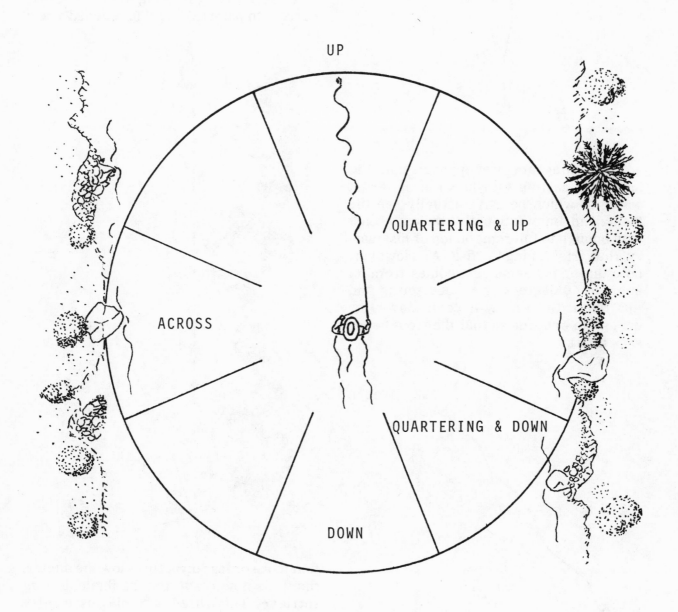

UP

QUARTERING & UP

ACROSS

QUARTERING & DOWN

DOWN

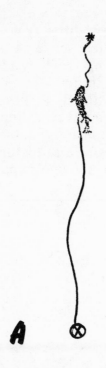

A

There is a classical way to present a fly such that it plays three roles on the same cast. The cast is made quartering and across stream to position (1), alighting in some form of current and then floating down to position (2) where the line comes taut, quartering and below the angler. This float is the first act of a three-act performance. If he wishes, the fisherman may lengthen the natural drift by feeding out extra line just before the fly comes to the end of its tether at (2). Otherwise, when held tight, the fly is going to swing across-current to point (3). Having reached a posi-

This diagram presupposes that the angler is casting into an area of target water in which he can't actually see the trout, and unintentionally, makes a cast long enough to fall right on top of his quarry, thus frightening the fish (A). However, note that if the same cast comes from an angle of 40 degrees or so, quartering and upstream, the line will come down far enough to one side so that the trout never sees it (B).

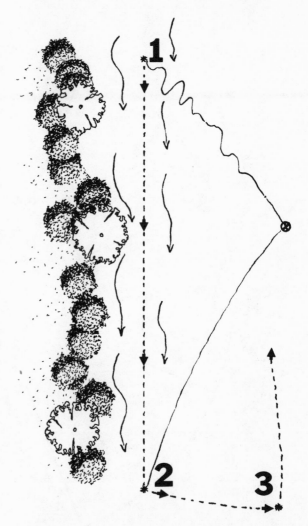

B

tion more or less directly below the angler, the fly is now ready for the finale, a drag retrieve. This three-part play is a nifty means of testing wet-fly presentations. As discussed more fully in later chapters, fly depth is frequently critical in wet-fly fishing. During the natural drift, the fly will

22

sink progressively until the line comes taut, submerging faster if the fly or leader is weighted or if the line is of the sinking variety. This is an excellent way to sample trout response at different depths. Then, during the swing, the fly will tend to rise again from bottom to top. This is precisely what certain nymphs do in the process of getting ready to hatch. The swing can be speeded by retrieving line while in progress, or it can be slowed by releasing line. There are enough options off this cast to keep an angler busy all day. The drag retrieve, in particular, offers all sorts of room for experimentation. The fly's return may be smooth and even or erratic and jerky, fast or slow, shallow or deep, and so on; the possibilities are nearly endless. Wet flies imitate four major kinds of food: land insects that have tumbled in, immature forms of aquatic insects, drowning adults following mating and egg laying, and finally, minnows. If there should be an abundance of feebly active nymphs awash in the currents or victims of drowning, look for best results on the dead drift component. Streamer fishermen dote on the swing segment where they make their fly dart across-current, minnow fashion, and at times the swing portion is especially deadly when it causes a bottom-to-top movement of the artificial in the manner of a hatching nymph. On still other occasions, the stream may abound with highly active, free-swimming nymphs, much to the delight of the drag retriever, and so it goes. This isn't a likely technique for dry fly fishing, for two of the three acts involve drag, although, on occasion, adult flies will water ski across the surface, dragging their tails in the process of laying eggs. Here the swing segment can be used to skate a floating imitation through the surface film in similar fashion.

While there are many advantages in casting across-stream at one angle or another, there is also a considerable potential for drag as compared with basically upstream casts. This hazard is proportional to the amount of current variation within the water the line must cross, or putting it differently, drag is a threat whenever your cast is made *from* or *across* current of one speed into target water of different velocity. Acceleration drag occurs when the back line or mid-part of the line gets caught in current that's faster than the water in the target area and bellies downstream, pulling the fly after it. Not only does the helpless fly zip off at a high rate of speed, but the angle of float changes abruptly as well, a combination that scares trout silly. Impedance drag is created by the reverse mix of currents wherein the back line gets mired in relatively slow water and functions like an anchor. Again there is a deviation of float angle, but this time, the fly puts on the brakes. These current diagrams are far more simple than many real stream situations because there are often three or even more current speeds to contend with, not to mention the very real possibility that adjacent currents will run in somewhat different directions! Nor do currents need to be very broad in order to create a problem; in fact, small water is especially challenging in this regard. The detailed surfaces of brooks and creeks are covered by slender, intertwined tongues of variable current, punctuated by pockets of quiet water, miniature waterfalls, and so on — a regular maze of threatening drag problems. There are specific casts designed to combat drag, as we shall see, but the easiest solution in many instances is to avoid crossing variable speed water in the first place. Currents tend to run in the same direction as the stream bed, and so current variation is least when the line is thrown more or less straight upstream. Then it is more likely that the angler will be standing in water with the same current velocity as that in his target. Correspondingly, cross-stream casts usually have the greatest potential for drag, admitting that there are good and sufficient reasons for fishing sidesaddle.

Ray Bergman made an extremely sound suggestion in his classic book, *Trout*, relative to "fishing out the cast." This applies to both drag retrieved and natural drifted flies and can be paraphrased: If the presentation is worth making at all, it is worth following to its completion. This means that a retrieved fly should be brought back to within a few feet of the fisherman as should a drifting fly, unless dragging or in danger of snagging. This is because trout commonly follow a fly for some distance before deciding to take, and may even strike on a now-or-never basis just as the fly accelerates on its way out of the water, drag notwithstanding. There is a natural tendency to lose interest in the fly after it has passed through the heart or best part of the target. At this point, the fisherman wants to get on with things, make a fresh cast, identify a new target, or whatever. This is surely a strong temptation, but there is little doubt that the few extra seconds of float or retrieve is time well spent. Unfortunately, like other pieces of advice, this one is easier to give than to follow. Every season, I manage to lose a number of fish by literally taking the fly away from them on the pickup.

In summary, the old orthodox dead drift is truly the most dependable presentation, and the angler who hasn't mastered it is at a huge disadvantage. Still, the crux of the matter, I think, is to avoid getting locked into any single method, even natural drifting. A friend recently scored heavily on the Conejos River in southern Colorado (in the midst of the Labor Day crowd, at that), by swinging his nymph across currents. Roughly 30 fish preferred the swing segment to dead drifts or direct drag retrieves, yet I've worked the identical water on a number of occasions with honors going heavily to the natural drift each time. What-

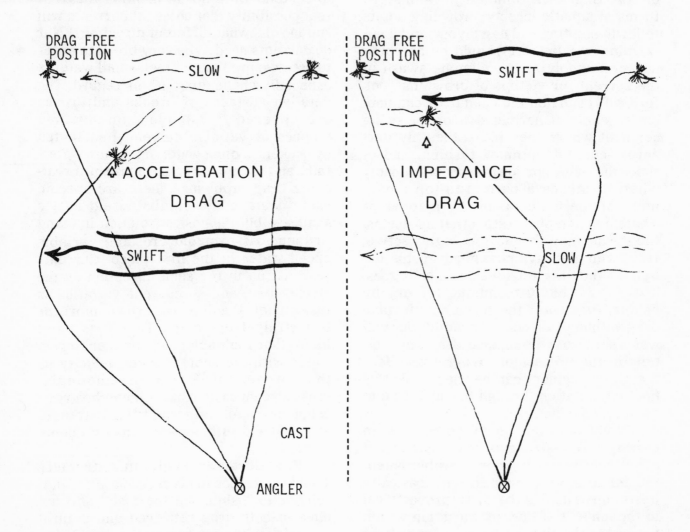

ever the reasons for these trout reactions, we can be sure that they are based on biological factors rather than chance. Deciding how you want your fly to behave in front of the finny audience mustn't be a rigid decision. It isn't a matter of going one way or the other as in making a major financial investment. I believe it's important to develop an open-minded, flexible attitude with an eye toward changing conditions. This is the best insurance possible against the continuing bad luck with which certain fishermen feel they are plagued!

APPROACHING

We have looked at two kinds of strategic decisions that anglers make again and again during the course of a day on the stream: selection of target water and type of presentation. The presentation you choose will go a long way toward determining how you position yourself in relationship to the target, whether below it, above it, or across stream from it. There is also a third important decision at hand, namely *proximity* to target water. How close can you or should you try to approach before casting? We know that trout come equipped with very sensitive "early warning systems," and that once frightened, they are not catchable for some time. Thus the trout have a clear-cut way of defining an approach that is *too* close. Common sense suggests that casts should be made from good safe distances, and indeed, beginners almost invariably adopt a super-cautious attitude in this regard. No doubt caution is commendable in any endeavor, up to a point, but many fearful learners overdo it and make things hard for themselves in the process. There are all sorts of dividends for an aggressive angler who likes to crowd the trout a bit. For one thing, close approaches mean shorter and hence less demanding casts, and further, the potential for drag is more or less proportional to the amount of line on the water, and so short throws are also desirable from this standpoint. In this regard there is another analogy to the game of golf that appeals to me. No matter how skilled or unskilled, any player is going to make a higher percentage of easy shots than hard ones. So why attempt a long difficult fly cast when you can get away with a "chip shot"? And quite apart from casting, flies are much easier to follow at close range in the interests of detecting strikes and setting hooks.

An aggressive approach may be well and good, but how do you know when you're overdoing it? Continuing failure to catch anything isn't exactly an ideal sort of indicator; there should be a more practical way to judge the amount of risk you're taking, and there is. It all has to do with reading the water. A clever reader can take immense liberties with the trout's highly developed alarm systems, and more exactly, he will key on cover. Cover is a two-way street in the sense that the same features and conditions that create cover for the trout also tend to disguise the fisherman's presence. For example, roily water hides each party from the other, but there is one very fundamental difference that works in favor of the fisherman. The angler has a potent selective advantage because he doesn't need to actually *see* the trout in order to catch them. Certainly, from time to time we do go after individual risers or fish that we spot beneath the surface; however, the majority of the trout I capture come from pieces of water I fish because they "read" as if they were worth working. Stated differently, an angler is perfectly content to fish promising water whether he can see the quarry or not, but the trout don't realize they are being stalked unless the fisherman does something to tip them off.

Solid cover objects such as rocks, beds of water weed, or submerged brush may provide an opportunity to move in right on top of unsuspecting fish; it's simply a matter of getting the cover between you and them. An elevated overhanging bank can be put to the same purpose by standing back out of sight while dapping the leader and fly over the edge. Meandering meadow streams are ideal dapping grounds in the tradition of the barefoot boy with his bent pin and grasshopper. Snake-like stream beds provide sharp curves and bends such that very short casts across the bank angle into hidden water on the other side are both safe and easy. These are devastatingly effective little tricks, sometimes to an extent that certain parts of a stream become virtual trout traps. I have fished a difficult little creek west of Colorado Springs often enough to become quite familiar with its many nooks and crannies. One tiny pool allowed me to take unfair advantage of the Browns that lived in it, thanks to a strategically placed boulder.

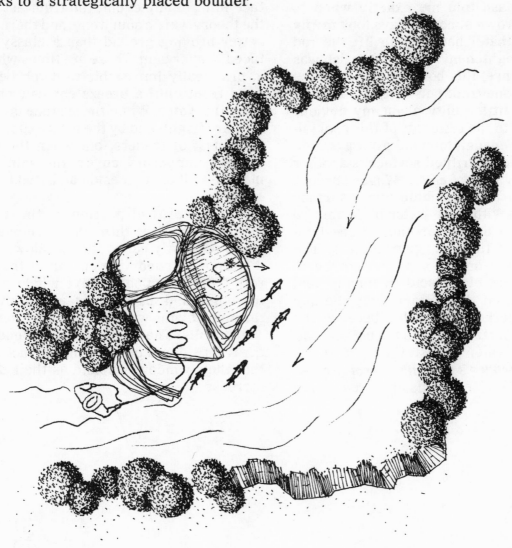

Picture a 12-foot-wide flow of perfectly clear water, seldom more than a foot deep and running between dense stands of tall willows. The stream was forced into a 90 degree turn by a high bluff, making the sharp cut around a big boulder some eight feet in height. A deep glide swept along the boulder's face and contained a half-dozen good fish, although they appeared to be completely uncatchable the first few times I tried for them. It was impossible to so much as peek around the rocky corner without spooking the wary Browns, let alone trying an upstream cast, and the willows took away the possibility of casting from either bank. I even tried to float my fly downstream from above, but another bend forced me in too close, and the trout scurried under their protective rock. As it turned out, the boulder was more of a traitor than a friendly place to hide. Its smooth surface sloped steeply down to the water in such a way that if I cast the last few feet of line on top of the big rock, the leader and fly would slowly roll down its face and right into the head of the glide.

I could do this from behind the big rock without showing myself or the rod, and although the fly was out of sight, a clearly audible splash told me exactly when to strike. A Brown almost always took my fly so deeply that I had only to lift the rod enough to tighten my line, and the fish was on. In essence, this boulder made me the present of one trout per visit, and I really felt just a little guilty about my devious dealings with the residents of this pool (although not enough to mend my ways).

A choppy or riffled surface is another double-duty kind of cover. Waves obscure the bottom and also hide above-surface detail from within the water by forming a multifaceted mirror, or more properly, a collection of tiny, merging mirrors. The usual comparison is to someone looking up at the surface of a placid swimming pool while lying on the bottom. Only the sky directly overhead is visible because the peripheral surface reflects the bottom, and should the water be disturbed, the entire surface becomes a dancing mirror. Frankly, I've never tried this in a real river except by accident, and on those few occasions, I was more concerned about drowning than with the optical physics of the surface film. In any event, the trout act as if the theory were a sound one, and there is no better proving ground than a glassy surfaced beaver dam. There are times when it is practically impossible to catch beaver pond trout until a breeze comes along to riffle the water. While the surface is quiet, they are frightened by the most expert cast and finest of leaders, but when the wind creates temporary cover, the same fish may toss all caution aside and strike ferociously.

The overhead portion of the swimming-pool surface through which one can see is popularly called the "window," as if it were a rounded area cut out of the mirror. Trout presumably have windows too, the angle and direction of which are determined by the way their eyes are set into their skulls. The window size depends on the trout's depth beneath the surface such that their windows expand as their depth increases.

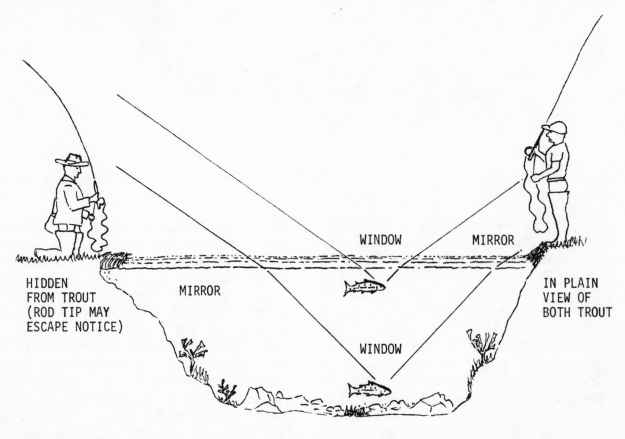

HIDDEN FROM TROUT (ROD TIP MAY ESCAPE NOTICE)

MIRROR

WINDOW   MIRROR

WINDOW

IN PLAIN VIEW OF BOTH TROUT

It's probably no accident that deep-swimming trout seem more secure than do those lying close to the surface (whether by design or because of shallow water). Top-siders are generally skittish and apprehensive. Of course, depth and surface texture may have opposing cover values as in the case of a shallow riffle. Nervous riffle feeders are at a real disadvantage with only a small window plus extensive mirroring of the surface, and they can be safely approached with considerable bravado.

It's obvious that the way in which an approach is made has a lot to do with how close one can get without spooking the fish, and this brings us back to the window. The circular wedge of space that encircles the window (peripheral to the mirror area) is blind to the trout, and it is consequently a safe portion of the "sky" for an angler to occupy. Naturally, there is a relationship between an angler's proximity to a given trout and that trout's window size, insofar as the approaching liberties he may take. However, in any situation it's better for the angler to stay *low*, because this helps keep him in the trout's blind zone. Although this sometimes means fishing from a crouch or from an uncomfortable kneeling position, it pays off! This is another reason why good fishermen are usually wading fishermen. A wader's profile is almost always going to be lower than that of an angler working from the bank. Casting a shadow over the fish is also fatal, and here again a low profile is desirable. Just as importantly, the dry-shod bank fisherman loses the majority of his positioning and approaching options, and I see no reason whatever to accept this sort of penalty as long as a stream is at all wadeable. If keeping your feet dry is more important than fishing properly, why not leave the rod at home and take up another hobby? Parenthetically, I am completely sold on some sort of fabric- or felt-soled footwear for wading. Rubber cleats just aren't adequate, and there is no sense in taking a dunking or serious fall when secure footing is so easily available. The felt-soled fisherman moves at least twice as quickly around the stream bed, and with much more confidence.

Small brushy streams and creeks pose the trickiest approaching problems, especially when the water is low and clear. Cramped into tight quarters, the fisherman needs to adopt some of the same stalking principles that are familiar to hunters. Keeping low is one of them, of course, and so is the avoidance of sudden jerky movements. Low, slow, and smooth are three good rules whether one is wading, casting, or just wiping a nose. Small stream work often forces an angler to wade because of fly-catching brush along the banks, and in thin, clear water he may become a victim of the "sentinel game." This infuriating phenomenon is the result of an effective if unintentional protective community effort on the part of the fish. Nearly all small waters have shallow bankside pockets containing tiny nursery shcool trout, and it's virtually impossible to aviod spooking these midgets as one wades along. Like sentinels, the pesky little fellows invariably scurry straight upstream into the middle of the pool or pocket you had planned to work next. Their precipitous arrival is sure to spread panic throughout the target area, ruining the water for as much as a half-hour. It's difficult to deal with sentinels although you can sometimes bushwhack along the banks to skirt them. I haven't found that fancy clothing camouflouge helps much, although there's not much sense in wearing bright, light colors that stand out starkly from the natural background. Larger waters require much less in the way of stealth, because the extra elbow room provides increased latitude for maneuvering around the target. The option of being able to cast from midstream toward the banks is a very useful example.

As noted in the preceding chapter, the upstream fisherman has already taken a giant step toward successful bold approaches by attacking the opponent's rear flank, but does this mean that he necessarily has to progress in an upriver direction? Not always. A fisherman may elect to walk downstream and still face up when he fishes his targets. The trouble is that he will have to skirt the water he wants to work widely enough so as not to frighten the fish, getting in below or across from each target. This continual circling process wastes time, and when the banks and stream bed are difficult to negotiate, walking down while fishing up amounts to doing things the hard way. An upstream angler can take on his targets in sequence as they come along, and all from the trout's blind backside at that. Correspondingly, you will find that most downstream anglers are either drag retrieving or using the three-part, drift-swing-drag sequence off a cross-stream cast.

There is a big difference between routinely fishing from the bank and taking selective advantage of what the bank position has to offer. Banks aren't all bad. Assuming that you can live with a high profile, the vantage from an elevated bank can make a small fly or feeding fish much more visible, and fly placement more precise. Part of this has to do with reduced glare and part with enhanced depth perception. A high bank once helped me pull off a bit of chicanery in the high meadows of the Fryingpan River, one of Colorado's greatest trout streams. I hadn't seen a rise since late morning on this September day; I was fording the river on my way back to the trail when, to my surprise, I spotted a half-dozen rings in a tight cluster at the tail of a shallow glide. I looked over the river carefully, but this appeared to be an isolated rise; there was no other evidence of activity on the river in either direction. The glide lay to one side of a strong channel current some 80 feet above me, and it presented a very tough casting challenge. I couldn't position myself much closer because of deep water, and the adjacent bank didn't look promising. It was packed with willows to the very edge. I was also afraid that the soft earth would transmit vibrations to the water should I trespass there. The only approach remaining required a 70-foot throw on a tangent across the central current. My cast would have to be accurate and yet fall with some slack in the end if a sickening

drag were to be prevented. I really doubted my ability to pull off this kind of performance. However, I also hated to give up on the last opportunity of the day, and so I continued to examine the situation. Then I noticed a jagged piece of bank that stood out in the fashion of a small platform some 18 inches above the water and about 30 feet below the rise rings; its surface was dotted by stunted willows separated by clumps of grass. Was it worth a try? Having nothing to lose, I inched almost to the edge on hands

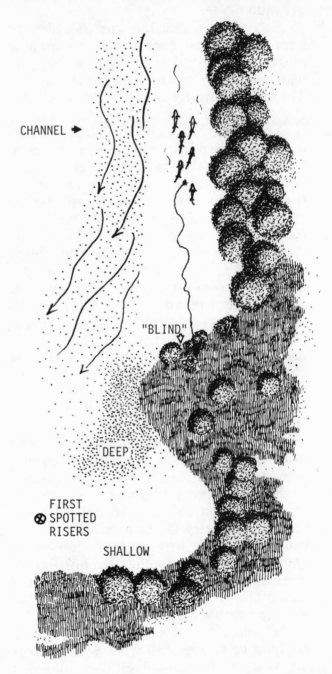

CHANNEL ➡

"BLIND"

DEEP

FIRST
⊗ SPOTTED
RISERS

SHALLOW

and knees so that the last tier of stubby willows provided a shield. There was no breeze, and I found that the cast was a "piece of cake" once I got the knack of clearing the willows behind me on the backcast from a kneeling position. Sure enough, the first time my no. 18 Royal Coachman fluttered down over the closest riser it was taken with complete confidence. The Brown dashed straight for my platform without interrupting his companions; I crawled to the rear, eased off into deep water and landed him in seclusion. In 30 minutes, I released three Browns between 12 and 15 inches in length from that identical spot and would have continued, if my knees and the rise hadn't worn out at about the same time.

I used to perform a somewhat peculiar although possibly informative experiment involving different approaching *philosophies*. The laboratory was a smallish stream that featured suspicious Browns in low clear water. My plan was to work this water in two different ways, as if I were two separate fishermen, during the same day. On the one hand, I would fish very carefully in a cautious, meticulous manner. Casts were planned and executed with all of the precision at my command after a stealthy approach, and I worked every piece of worthwhile water, no matter how difficult the required cast might be. The "other" fisherman emphasized getting his fly over as many trout as possible in the shortest period of time, making his approaches quickly, and crowding dangerously close while firing casts with reckless abandon. This greedy fellow walked right past difficult targets in search of quick rewards. I alternated these "Jeckel and Hyde" roles every two hours, keeping score all the while. Now you might reasonably suppose that the precise fisherman would come out ahead, and yet he seldom got so much as a tie. Although his crude opponent surely spoiled more water through speedy, daring approaches, a good many more trout got to see his fly in the first place. Further, in the process of tackling tough assignments, the fastidious fisherman frequently hung up his fly in the brush, thus failing to score and losing time, too. On this stream, the fast and furious approach was more efficient than the slow cautious one; however, this situation may easily reverse itself. The more disciplined attitude is not only commendable for the person who is trying to improve his skills, it's also the only way to catch fish under really difficult conditions.

The fisherman continually walks a fine line between a healthy respect for the trout's natural wariness and too much caution, which leads to inefficiency. Most beginners tend to be excessively respectful—learn to take some chances, it's fun to pull a fast one now and then. I've found it best to begin the day approaching aggressively, because I would rather err on that side of the fence. If things work out, so much the better. Other wise, when water that should produce doesn't, or if I see startled fish repeatedly running for cover, I gradually back off. Incidentally, fishing out the cast can be helpful in assessing the trout's timidity. If you get a number of strikes close in, they probably aren't particularly spooky and you can proceed accordingly.

FEARLESS FLY-CASTING

Beginners are frequently awed by fly-casting's reputation as a super-skill. I've seen them tense up with a fly rod like some poor duffer teeing off on the 16th at Pebble Beach in front of national television. In truth, there is very little analogy between the ordinary fly-cast and a golf stroke. The fisherman's essential moving parts are his elbow and wrist, and two joint motions can't require a whole lot of co-ordination. However, as those of us in the higher scoring brackets can attest, a full golf swing involves synchronization of a good many pieces of anatomy!

It's not necessary to be able to write one's initials with the line in mid-air in order to catch trout. There's a big difference between practical, productive fly-casting and exhibition performances. While not attempting to put the professional casters down, I often wonder just how much of an edge they would really have in the usual stream situation. Very long casts featuring extreme accuracy win ribbons, but they are neither necessary nor even desirable under routine circumstances. As a matter of fact, I favor unimpressive, little crooked casts because they are such great trout takers. Certainly, fly casting does require a bit of practice, but I'm convinced that poor catches are seldom the result of inept casting. Rather, there are a number of other failed or poorly performed skills that more often lead to bad fishing luck, so-called.

I want to make two points of explanation before getting underway: in the interests of simplicity, assume that the rod, line, leader, and fly are properly balanced and that the various casts described are being performed by a right-handed person such that the right hand holds the rod while the left is free to handle line.

For purposes of a low-pressure introduction to fly casting, I use what I call the metronome method. The rod is held by "shaking hands" with the grip, in friendly fashion, thumb on top. Then, holding the rod in *front* of him (or her; "hers" are just as adept) at a 60 degree angle from the horizontal, the student simply swings the rod back and forth, right to left, with about 15 feet of line out, plus a short leader and fly. In this way, he can watch the rod, line, leader, and fly all work together as a unit. Most people get a lasting impression of line and leader action as they coil and uncoil after just a couple of minutes. While this is going on, and without stopping the metronome, I suggest that the student feed out extra line with his left hand and then pull it back in, just as fishermen lengthen and shorten their lines on the stream. After a few minutes, it seems perfectly natural when the direction of rod travel is changed from side to side to the normal forward-and back-casting plane. Now the beginner is essentially false casting, or keeping his fly continually airborne, as he will later when drying a fly. Next the student is asked to stop the rod abruptly at the end of one of its forward swings, and he sees a nice straight cast unfold. He can be given the happy assurance that this modest effort is sufficient to catch plenty of trout and that he is ready for at least limited combat. Indeed, I was outfished one evening recently by a fellow who had never held a fly rod before! I spent about 10 minutes with him on the bank going through the metronome exercise until he seemed pretty facile and was making reasonable forward casts. I wanted to get in some fishing myself before dark, and so pointing out several practice targets in bankside water, I waded out toward mid-river. I was hardly underway when a frantic shout brought me to an abrupt halt. Fearing he had fallen, I spun around. To my relief, my friend was scrambling up the bank on all fours in pursuit of a flopping Rainbow. After a congratulatory wave, I continued on, and had negotiated a few more yards of fast water when another yell penetrated the roar of the current. I turned in time to see trout number two on proud display. When I was finally ready to make a cast of my own, he was cranking out 35 footers toward scattered rise rings, and as I watched in mild amazement, he took number three! Thus was born a new fly fisherman.

The old clock face diagram so commonly used for describing rod position during a cast is hard to beat. An angler is imagined to be standing in front of a giant dial with the rod in the place of a single hand. He faces 9:00, and 12:00 is straight overhead, so that during the false casting exercise the rod sweeps an arc more or less between 10:00 and 2:00. This is a fine way to show front and back rod position, but the clock face doesn't indicate whether the rod is held vertically or tipped sideways. As seen head on, many fly casters feel most comfortable with the rod tilted 10 degrees or so from the vertical toward the casting-arm side. The basic cast begins with the rod at 10:00, continues into the backcast until the 1:00 position is reached, and then enters the forward-cast segment of the sequence. The forward cast is completed with the rod stopping at about 9:30 as the line flies forward.

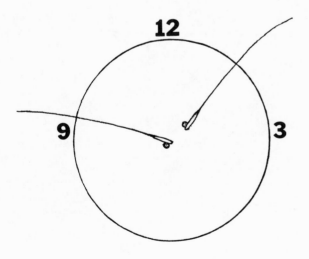

It's important to understand how the wrist and elbow interact during a cast, and in order to demonstrate this, I like to use two maneuvers that may seem pointless at first. Either the wrist or elbow can manage the basic cast alone, and so I ask the student to try this by first pretending his wrist is held rigid, as if in a plaster cast. The result is a very awkward, stiff presentation, but the cast can be made. Next, the elbow is immobilized in a bent position so that the wrist has to travel through an arc of about 100 degrees in carrying out the backcast and forward cast. He is then asked to compare these extremes with the combination of wrist and elbow movement that feels most natural. Everyone readily agrees that the combination is much easier than either "single joint" cast, and most learners will spontaneously flex their wrists back and forth through about 25 degrees during the cast without specific instruction. The point is that while the backcast should be a brisk, smooth, continuous movement, the forward cast isn't so uniform. This is because the wrist does most of its uncocking during the middle part of the rod movement as the rod passes from approximately 12:00 to 10:30 on its trip forward. These few degrees of wrist snap (I say "snap" because the uncocking takes place very quickly) impart a great deal of power or drive to the forward-flying line, much more than can be obtained through the efforts of either joint alone. In his book, *A Flyfisher's Life*, Charles Ritz adroitly compared this aspect with the way in which the wrist and elbow cooperate when driving a nail. The wrist can tap in a carpet tack by itself, but if one is hammering home a stout nail, both joints contribute, and neither runs the show. As noted, most beginners cock their wrists about 25 degrees on the backcast, returning to the original zero or "hand shaking" position at the conclusion of the forward cast. This is an appropriate amount of wrist action, and there's no need to fret over precisely how many degrees of flexion go into your cast. However, rod position at the conclusion of the backcast is very important. Good position is somewhere between 12:30 and 1:30, the rod should *not* wander any further back. If your rod sweeps all the way to 2:00 or 3:00, the backcast line will likely dip so low that the fly scrapes water or the ground behind the angler. If there are potential snags around, the fly usually manages to find them, leading to an interruption in operations. Too many of these little unsnagging trips can spoil your temper and do nothing to improve your catch.

Snags notwithstanding, it's difficult to launch a good forward cast when the rod is too far back. There is a loss of power or distance potential (especially when casting into wind), the fly tends to slap down hard on the target instead of landing gently, and accuracy may be impaired as well. Unfortunately, bad backcast position comes naturally. As a matter of fact, the rod feels comfortable back there between 2:00 and 3:00. For that matter, the resulting cast actually looks superficially fluid and graceful, providing the fly doesn't spank the water or get hung up. The culprit is usually an overly flexed wrist, back-cocked to 70 degrees or so.

There are several remedies, the simplest being to periodically remind yourself that 1:00 is far enough, and I'd even suggest shooting for 12:30 to be on the safe side. It's also a good idea to supplement the mental checks with an occasional over-the-shoulder glance to see where the rod really is. Ray Bergman's neat trick of running the index finger up on top of the rod grip instead of the thumb is also very helpful. You'll find that this grip discourages excessive back-flexing of your wrist, for it's very difficult to get the rod back into bad position without help from the wrist. Still, I've yet to see an angler who doesn't forget the 1:00 rule from time to time, I know I do, particularly after a long day of fly casting, when my arm is tired. Taking the rod back too far is the most common bad casting habit to which fishermen are prone, and each of us needs to guard against it.

A tardy forward cast, initiated too late after completion of the backcast, also allows the fly to drop to the surface, but oddly enough, this is an uncommon sort of mistake. In practice, the opposite tendency

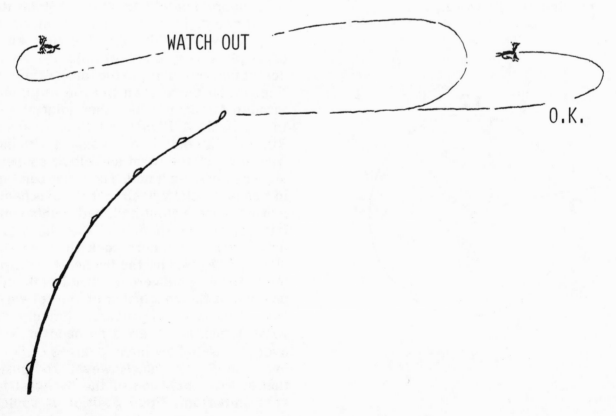

WATCH OUT

O.K.

prevails—that is, a premature forward cast wherein the rod reverses direction while the line is still tightly coiled, not having had time to straighten out on the backcast. This leads to "bull whipping," an unfortunate situation in which the angler actually plays crack-the-whip with his fly. This is an exasperating and an expensive game, because the sharp crack that accompanies the beginning of the forward cast often signals the departure of your fly from the end of the leader and "into orbit." Experience brings a second sense as to just where the fly is in relation to leader and line at any point in a cast sequence; however, beginners do well to twist around for an occasional visual check, just as in watching rod position. It is perfectly safe to begin the forward cast while the *end* of the terminal tackle is still in a loose loop— but beware the tightly coiled line and leader!

An old tradition holds that the caster should pause at the completion of the backward rod movement until he feels a little tug, indicating that the line has come straight on the backcast. In reality, a definite tug may never come along, so I recom-
time line is picked up for a new cast.
top of the backcast (plus an occasional backward glance) to guard against bull whipping. Although veteran fly casters go from the backcast into the forward cast in one fluid motion, beginners should try the pause. Your casting may not look as smooth, but at $.75 to $1 per fly, who cares?

I have largely ignored the left hand up to now, aside from its role in lengthening and shortening the line while false casting. However, fly casting is very much of a two-handed proposition. The left hand makes an important contribution each time line is picked up for a new cast. As in the metronome exercise, the left hand has a grip on the line fairly close to the lowest guide on the rod shaft, so that as the right hand takes the rod back, the left can simultaneously pull in a foot or so of forward line. This combination or rod lift plus left-hand line retrieval results in acceleration of the backcast, causing the line to fairly leap off the water. This is critical for the dry-fly fisherman who wants his fly to leave the surface quickly and cleanly. Otherwise, it will rip along in the surface film, creating an alarming wake and getting soaked in the bargain. All competent fly casters use their left hands for this purpose, it's more habit than skill. The left hand speeds up or slows down the line in several specific casts, to be discussed presently, and also provides a means of fine adjustment of cast length as in the "almost cast." This is simply a matter of false casting the fly a foot or so above the target without allowing it to touch the surface. When extreme accuracy is needed, final adjustments in both distance and direction can be made before the cast is permitted to sit down. It's like giving a golfer an opportunity to pull his ball back for another shot seconds before it lands in a sand trap or water hazard. This is one of the reasons that fly casting is less demanding than many suppose. Think what an "almost" golf shot would do for your score!

Apart from drying a fly or trying a cast on for size, I like to false cast while moving over short distances into new positions. It's less bother than reeling in, catching the fly and putting line out all over again, but don't get hung up on false casting, it can become a nervous habit. I remember one fellow who appeared to be an elegant fly caster, and yet he was surprisingly ineffective when it came to catching fish. When I watched him closely, I found that his artificial was airborne most of the time because *more than 95 percent* of his casts were of the false variety. The flying trout is a very rare species!

Although the standard cast described thus far will usually get your fly where you want it, there are a number of common variations that come in handy.

Line shooting is a valuable means of simplifying medium and long range casts by allowing the fisherman to false cast less line than the completed cast calls for. This is convenient when the backcast has to be curtailed because of nearby brush, etc. Since the line has weight plus velocity, it tugs strongly against the rod tip at the completion of a crisp forward cast. There are usually several loops of loose line between the left hand and the reel, and so if the left hand releases its hold just before the forward cast comes taut and pulls against the rod, the momentum of the forward-flying line will pull out these loops, essentially adding them to the cast. A shorter line is always the easiest to handle on any sort of cast, and like many anglers, I almost routinely shoot a little slack whether there are rearward obstructions or not. For example, slack inevitably accumulates on upstream presentations and is retrieved and stored by the left hand in these loose coils. I pick up the fly when it's close to me on a short line, false cast a time or two, and simply reshoot the stored slack. If I shoot six feet of line on a 30-foot cast, it only shortens my false cast or backcast by 25 percent (assuming that rod length accounts for another six feet out of the total). This may not sound significant, but the difference in handling ease is considerable, and there should be little if any loss of accuracy.

Single and double haul casts are designed to deliver extreme distance, utilizing the principle of mid-flight line acceleration. This is accomplished by pulling in several feet of line with the left hand while the forward cast or backcast is in progress. The resultant kick-up in line speed is something akin to shifting into passing gear. When the left hand releases its grip just in time for the shoot, the increment in velocity is sufficient to take out the segment that was pulled in as well as a good deal more. In the double haul, extra line is actually shot into an extended backcast, followed immediately by a second left-hand haul during the forward cast. As you might suppose, these professional-appearing tricks require careful timing and a clever left hand. At least at first, I'd leave the hauls for the fancy fly casters armed with their specially weighted shooting lines backed by light monofilament. I can't remember really *having to* double haul during the past ten seasons, even in fishing some pretty big rivers. As noted in the introduction, spinning is a logical solution for extreme distance work anyway.

Slack-line casts are the real secret to success in water with drag problems. The idea is to get the end of the line and leader to fall in a wavy or serpentine form so that drag prone currents will first straighten out the curves, semiloops, and squiggles before wrenching at the fly. Putting contortions into the line and leader while still dropping the fly on target is a knack that takes practice, although it isn't necessarily difficult from a technical standpoint. Many beginners are rather put off by the concept of slack casts. They had rather make long straight throws like the tournament casters. In baseball lingo, the short, dumpy slack casts might be likened to knuckle balls, off-speed, and various "junk" pitches, as opposed to the screaming fast ball or sharp breaking curve. However, these junk casts win most of the games we play with trout in difficult fast water. Here a ruler-straight 45-footer that provides only one second of drag-free drift is much less effective than a crooked 20-foot cast with five seconds of natural drift built in.

People neither talk nor write much about slack-line casting, perhaps because it is difficult to describe. There are several basic approaches. The first might be called an "out of gas" forward cast, implying that there is hardly any wrist snap. The rod is brought forward in a lazy, almost tired fashion with the result that the line and leader aren't given enough drive to straighten out. Then there is the platform concept wherein one tries to cast his fly onto an *imaginary surface* six feet or so *above* the water. Normally, the rod reaches 9:30 as it lays out the forward cast, but this time it stops at about 11:00 for an "up-hill" delivery such that the force of the cast dissipates while the terminal tackle is still airborne, high above the surface. As before, the line and leader tend to fall in a series of tiny curves and partial loops. Ritz described a third and closely related manuever which he descriptively called the parachute cast. This one is performed with an extended, semi-straightened elbow. At the completion of the forward cast, your hand is above your head, rather than at the normal shoulder level, with the rod pointing toward 10:30. The line's energy fails long before the fly can alight, and as soon as the line goes dead, the whole arm drops suddenly to belt level. This causes the fly to flutter or parachute down like the proverbial wounded duck. As you can see, elements of each of the three methods can be combined. Finally, it is often helpful to shoot some slack into the forward cast, but *more* than the line drive can straighten out. Beginners always fret when they are unable to get their line and leader to fall nice and straight. They shouldn't. After all, this could be a natural and most useful talent if cultivated! Indeed, I've gotten into the habit of putting at least a little slack into almost every cast I make just as insurance against unseen drag problems. Incidentally, you'll find that a little breeze blowing in your face is a big help in casting slack, while a following wind makes things harder by ironing out those line-leader wrinkles.

Side-arm casts are useful for getting a fly under overhanging brush via a low trajectory and also for fighting the wind. Some anglers worry that if the rod is held straight up they will rap the fly against the rod shaft. In addition to tilting the rod away from the vertical a little, their casting hand circles ever so slightly as it travels back and forth to avoid possible rod rapping. In any event, there is no law to the effect that the rod should be mostly vertical, and at times it is advantageous to go with a three-quarter delivery in the manner of a side-arm pitcher with the rod at an angle of 45 degrees or even parallel to the water surface. The backcast in this situation will naturally be low, and so the rear should be free of obstructions, although this is a neat means of zipping a fly in under overhanging brush. Wind velocity is frequently least just above the water surface and this is why these flat casts are such effective wind cheaters. Line can also be driven with extra force when wind is a problem by increased arm and wrist effort. At times, it's even necessary to throw some shoulder and body into the forward cast by shifting your weight in the manner of a boxer throwing a punch. Under extreme conditions, line velocity can be futher increased

to give it more wind-cutting potential by hauling in a couple of feet with the left hand as the line rockets forward.

The cross-body cast is a method for avoiding obstructions along the bank when the bank is on the same side as your casting arm and it's impossible or undesirable to move into the center of the stream. Twisting the torso at an angle away from the bank, the casting arm is held across the angler's chest so that the right hand stops in front of the left shoulder on the backcast. The line unfolds behind him and away from the bank toward mid-stream while the forward cast comes in low, from left to right, as his trunk untwists. This isn't the kind of cast you want to make all day long, but it's great for tight spots and for dealing with cross winds that would otherwise deposit the fly in the trees, if not in your ear!

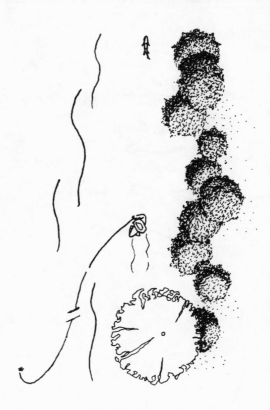

Curve casts are used to damp out drag when throwing to a target on the opposite side of a strong current, and also to avoid "lining" a trout. In the first instance if you can get the line to fall in a curve with the bulge facing upstream across the current, the natural float will be protected until the current eventually reverses the curve. Even after this happens, you may be able to *mend* the curve by flicking the line back upstream with the rod tip, being careful not to disturb the fly.

As noted above, fly fishers live in horror of lining their quarry. To this end, if the last part of the line and leader can be bent to one side to form a shallow letter "J," the line and thick part of the leader will float down to one side of the trout while the fly stays on a course such that it passes right over his nose. A right hander throws a right curve by holding the rod somewhat side-arm while making an out-of-gas forward cast. The amount of curve can be adjusted by varying line speed and rod tilt. A fairly upright rod gives a shallow little bend while a big fat "U" can be created with a flatter rod angle. Left curves can be managed off a lazy, left-to-right, cross-body cast. I sometimes throw a left curve by coming sideways across my chest from right to left and adding a short, sharp, left-hand pull or haul just before the fly hits the water. There is no shoot, but the added acceleration literally drives the fly into a shallow left curve as it dives in low and fast, sneaking under brush along the left bank.

The *steeple cast* is a favorite means of kicking the backcast way up high in order to clear rearward obstructions in circumstances where you're forced to stand closer than is comfortable. On an ordinary cast, the right hand comes back chin high while the upper arm and shoulder are relatively immobile. In the steeple technique, the wrist and partially straightened elbow let

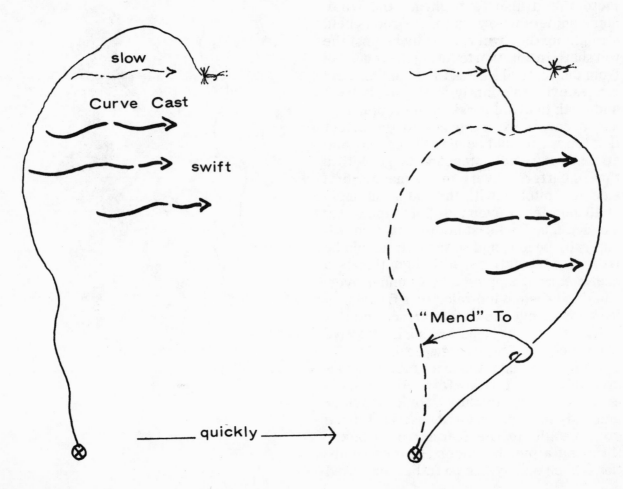

slow

Curve Cast

swift

quickly

"Mend" To

the shoulder take over a lot of the motion such that the entire arm becomes an extension of the rod, and the casting hand ends up over the angler's head at the top of the backcast. The rod stops at 12:30, and so the plane of the cast tilts into a low-in-front to high-in-back axis, causing the line to fly more up than back. The result is a short, high backcast. You can false cast with the steeple technique, although the fly will slap the water in front if you aren't careful. I commonly use a partial steeple cast that is halfway between the standard and fully extended arm method by partially straightening my elbow and bringing my hand back above eye level.

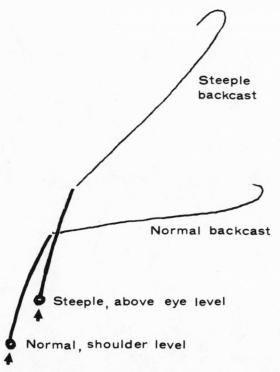

Steeple backcast

Normal backcast

Steeple, above eye level

Normal, shoulder level

HAND POSITION, TOP OF BACKCAST

The *roll cast* goes back to a trick most of us learned as kids, changing the position of the lawn sprinkler. It was much more fun to move the sprinkler by rolling loops of hose toward it than turning off the water and resetting it. That was too much like work, as I recall. The dependable roll cast is nothing more than a snappy forward cast made while the front part of the line is *still on the water*. As the rod is slowly raised to the usual 1:00 position, it lifts the rear seg-

ment of the line from the surface, and as the rod rocks forward, that segment becomes a rolling loop, just like the hose. This loop not only moves precisely in the direction dictated by the rod, but also travels along the length of the line until it eventually incorporates the leader. Reaching the fly, the loop opens and disappears, and as it does so, the fly is deposited right on target. This cast is highly accurate, simple to perform, free of fatigue, and requires no backcast whatever. It is necessary that the back part of the line be at the angler's feet when the roll is initiated, but casts of 30 feet or more are perfectly possible by straightening and raising your casting arm to the 1:00 position (as in the steeple cast) in order to lift up a larger loop. By roll casting from a side-arm position, the fly can be delivered on a low, brush-cheating trajectory, and this facet, coupled with the freedom from backcast worries, makes the roll cast an invaluable aid on brushy water. I once spent an entire day pinned between deep water and dense thickets of giant bramble bushes in the desert canyon of Idaho's Big Wood River. I needed to get the fly out about 40 feet, but I was already at the brink of unwadeable water, and sharp thorns were ripping my jacket and stinging my back. The trick was to pile up loose coils of line at my feet like a harpooner and let fly with a hard, extended-arm roll cast. This form of line delivery has plenty of power for wind fighting, and while I use it for both wet- and dry-fly work, it is magnificent for casting weighted wet flies. Formal overhead casts with weighted flies are inaccurate and even dangerous, and so I use the roll almost exclusively when fishing them, often going through an entire day without making a single standard cast!

The single most irritating catastrophe that can befall an innocent angler occurs when he inadvertently moves into casting position with a bush or tree directly behind him. The backcast unavoidably sails into the teeth of a forest of snags, and the outcome is highly predictable. For some reason, this sort of accident has a way of repeating itself all day long and we might conclude that the victim is either stupid or careless, or a little of both. However, I'm sure it's just a matter of inexperience. For instance, drivers who are used to heavy traffic develop a sense of who and what is behind them and on either flank without really thinking about it or looking frequently. Veteran fly fishermen seem to do the same, seldom getting hung up behind unless they are done in by an errant gust of wind or when they miss while attempting to set the hook on a strike. "Look before you cast" is an irritatingly trite little motto, but I would also commend the steeple, cross-body, and roll casts as a means of avoiding "hangups."

After so much talk about steeple, parachute, shooting, rolling, and curving casts, I'm afraid the reader may be perplexed—and this is exactly what I want to avoid. Try fooling around with these various casting suggestions on the lawn for a little while. I like the term "fooling around" because it's low key, and that is how your casting should be—why make a relatively easy thing difficult?

FLY RODS

It's no wonder beginners get perplexed over selection of their first fly rod when you think of the variables that are involved. A decision is in order as to the rod's length, its weight, type of action, the number of joints, brand, price, whether to buy a pure fly rod or a fly-spin combination, and so on. Some choices such as bamboo versus synthetic (fiberglass or graphite) are of the either/or sort, while others present an impressive range of options. For instance, you may elect to pay as little as $15 or as much as $350 for an adequate rod. The problem is to sort out these many factors into some order of priority as to their individual importance. One variable to which we can all relate is money, and while this is an eminently practical issue, fortunately it's one that can come last.

A fly rod's soul is in its "action," if an inanimate object can be said to have such. In reality, a fly rod does have life, for the angler can surely feel it react under his hand, and there's no doubt that different rods feel differently. Nonetheless, rod action is very hard to define, no matter how many adjectives and synonyms we dredge up. I suppose that the two closest would be "springiness" and "suppleness," although neither term is really satisfactory. A visual definition based on a demonstration I once watched is more useful. Two rods with contrasting actions were placed with their grips held securely in a carpenter's vise such that the shafts extended horizontally, parallel to the floor. A six-ounce sinker was then tied to the tip guide of each rod by means of a string, almost touching the floor. The first rod was one with *slow action*, and it displayed a slight downward bend under its own weight, even before the sinker weight was attached. Weighted, it described a smooth arc from the deeply bowed tip clear back almost to the cork grip. The second rod was one with *fast action*; and with the sinker attached, it

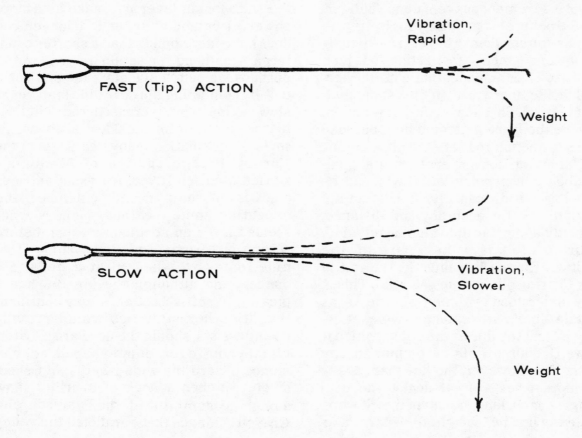

FAST (Tip) ACTION — Vibration, Rapid — Weight

SLOW ACTION — Vibration, Slower — Weight

dropped its tip relatively little, showing no bend at all beyond the mid-shaft.

When the strings were severed, both rods began to vibrate up and down, but in clearly different ways. The slow-action rod's vibrations looked slow, and it took a number of seconds for the shaft to become still in its original unweighted position. The other rod's vibrations were shallow and rapid, quickly fading as it returned to its rigid position, almost like a piece of spring steel. Thus there was a sharp contrast between the full-length, *supple,* buggy-whip action of the slow-action rod and the *springy* resiliency of the stiffer, fast-action rod.

The point of all this is that most of us cast much better if we can feel the rod flex down in the grip, not that there is an actual flex in the grip itself, but the slightest bend in the lower shaft does in fact come across to your hand. This is true to an extent that experienced fly casters have the sensation that the rod is a living extension of their hand, like a very long finger. Since the rod is flexed by the line, with leader and fly following dependably along, this feeling of control is a tremendous confidence builder. Imagine being able to place your fly as precisely as you can point a finger! Due to their rigid lower segments, fast-action rods lack this sense of communication with the terminal tackle; there just isn't the same feeling of control. So, one vote for slow action, but here the issue gets muddied, because while slow-action rods are the ultimate for "feel" they fall down in another vital quality called *power potential.* Power can be defined as a rod's capacity to cast an appropriate line for accuracy and distance, especially against or into significant wind. "Appropriate" is a key part of the definition, for the line must fit the rod in order to bring out its true potential. This is easily understood by thinking of the rod as a simple, single-arm catapult (which it actually is) and the line as the object which it throws. Of course the fly caster puts energy into the rod; however, the line that he sets into motion has a great deal to do with springing or cocking the catapult, as it were. Should the line be too light for a particular rod, its pull will be insufficient to cock the catapult enough to make it come alive. A poorly sprung fly rod makes a feeble catapult, for no matter how much inherent power it may have, a rod can't perform adequately until it is activated. By the same token, if the line is too heavy and its pull too great, the rod will be over-sprung or buckled, again performing poorly in the manner of an overloaded catapult. Wind comes into the picture because it brings out and strongly emphasizes a fly rod's power or lack of same. Armed with reasonable equipment, a competent fly caster can make beautiful long casts, even if his rod is down on power, providing the wind isn't against him. But let a good stiff breeze come up, and his efforts will begin to suffer in a big way, for he will no longer be able to put the fly where he wants it with any consistency. As you might expect, a fast springy rod loaded with a relatively heavy, wind-cutting line is a potent tool for dealing with buffeting breezes, while a good-feeling, slow-action rod can become an outright liability. And so, we are faced with a dilemma—but what about rod length? Doesn't a longer lever arm make for a more powerful catapult? Indeed, a longer rod does have more punch than a shorter counterpart matched for action quality, and so perhaps we can "have our cake and eat it too" by combining the desirable features of slow action with increased rod length. I learned a rather physical lesson about this sort of combination many years ago in the Varney Bridge section of Montana's storied Madison River. It was an ominous overcast morning in mid-September, and expecting some weather, I chose what seemed to be an adequate weapon before setting out from West Yellowstone. This nine-footer weighed in at a hefty 5¼ ounces, and although the big rod had a pleasingly softish action, I was confident that its other statistics would provide power assists, should the need arise. Later, clambering over dome-shaped cobblestones toward the wide river, I apprehensively watched a flock of swirling snow along the summits of the Madison and Gravelly Ranges that paralleled the valley on either side. It wasn't long before a strong, frigid breeze began to blow steadily down the Madison valley as if it were a wind tunnel. To my dismay, I found that the long rod had to be extended to its fullest in order to get out any line at all. My buggy whip was so bowed at the top of the backcast that its tip wasn't far from my casting hand. Even when I ripped the rod back and forth almost flat to the surface, I could seldom propel the fly as far as 20 feet. Sometimes it landed behind me or embedded itself in my hat or jacket, and it had to be painfully extracted from my right ear on several occasions. It would have been sensible to give up, but, after all, one has only so many days to spend on meccas such as the Madison in an ordinary lifetime. Hours later, when I stumbled back to the car, dusted by snowflakes and shivering in the gathering darkness, seven Browns and an accommodating Whitefish had been released, although my back, casting shoulder, and hand felt as if I had spent the day arm wrestling (and losing). Thus I discovered that action is a more important determinant of rod power than length or weight.

I'm sure the reader has long since perceived that a rod with *medium* action might be a sensible solution to the feel versus power conflict. This is indeed the case. There is no reason that a rod has to be manufactured such that it displays either extreme of action, and there is a whole spectrum available from the slowest to the fastest. Medium action is an exceptionally practical compromise, offering reasonable power potential and letting the hand know what the terminal tackle is doing at the same time.

I rate rod length as the next most important characteristic. Ten-footers, once commonplace, are now curiosities because of a continuing trend toward shorter fly rods. Seven-footers were considered stubby 25 years ago, while today's midgets are down to five feet or so, and the seven-foot rod has become standard. Retailers have been pushing shorter rods pretty hard, and I really suspect that there is a simple commercial principle involved.

With proper care, a fly rod should enjoy a long life, and further, most anglers already own a satisfactory rod of "normal" length, but if the fly fishing public can be convinced that little five-foot wands are something special, a whole new market opens up. In my view, these delicate creations are great for packing through the brush, but this is their prime virtue. Length is a significant, if secondary, consideration in determining a rod's power potential, and this applies to the roll cast as well as to standard overhead presentations. The roll is highly dependent on rod length for leverage. Indeed, a few inches make a noticeable difference such that an eight-foot rod is superior to a seven-footer. I used to look forward to fishing a very brushy tributary of the Big Laramie River in northern Colorado which harbored fat Brownies, hidden in a veritable jungle of willows. The leafy vegetation formed a complete canopy over the water, usually making any form of backcast impossible. Still, by employing a good bit of stealth and wading in a crouch, it was possible to get within 20 feet of the fearful fish. At this range, I could drop a fly gently over them by means of a low-flying, side-arm roll cast. This was the kind of challenge one thinks about on snowy winter evenings, and during a fit of January madness, I convinced myself that I absolutely had to have a tiny rod in order to fish this stream properly. To this end, I purchased a costly bamboo-rod kit from which I constructed a wispy 6½-foot beauty, equipping it with a delicate new line. When the long-awaited day for its initiation arrived, I was fortunate enough to be blessed by sunny skies, low clear water, and rising trout on all sides. The tiny rod was a joy to carry through the willow maze as anticipated —but the rest was all bad news. I simply couldn't roll cast enough line to reach most of the Brownies, no matter how carefully and daringly I approached. In addition, when I was able to get off an overhead cast, the unaccustomed rod length threw off my timing and I continually underestimated the height of my backcasts, ending up in the willows time and again. I was more than just disappointed, for there went a winter's worth of hopes down the drain, not to mention a significant financial investment. I returned the following morning, armed with an old, inexpensive eight-foot glass rod and was able to triple the previous day's catch, almost entirely on the basis of improved rod performance.

It might seem that small streams and short rods should go together, but the reverse is often true. A rod of reasonable length greatly assists in roll casting, keeping the backcast high, dapping a fly over the bank or around a rock, and is invaluable for lifting the rear part of the line free of drag-prone currents (as discussed more fully in the upcoming chapter on slack-line control).

Rod weight is not extremely critical and has no relationship whatever to action. Fly rods other than the light graphites generally fall into a narrow range between 3 and 4½ ounces anyway. Insofar as casting fatigue is concerned, rod weight is hardly worth worrying about in comparison with action. Slow rods, not necessarily the heavy ones, require the most muscle to keep the line airborne. The fairy-wand cult takes pride in one-ounce creations with the idea that ultra-light rods make landing a trout more thrilling. Surely it takes a dainty rod to get much play out of a small trout, but it seems to me that this should be a very secondary kind of consideration. You have to hook them before you can play them!

Durability, money, and esthetics are the three issues involved in choosing between bamboo and synthetic fiber rods. Bamboo rods are clearly the tougher and more likely to survive a bang in the screen door or snub against a tree trunk than hollow, shatter-prone fiber rods. I'm reminded of an unintentional although rather elegant experiment that demonstrated this pretty convincingly. The power-driven rear window of a station wagon was closed on two rod tips of similar diameter resting a half-inch apart, one glass and the other bamboo. The glass tip snapped like a dry twig, while its bamboo companion escaped undamaged. I should know, since I was the one who performed this dumb trick by turning the key backward in the rear-window lock!

There used to be a price differential between bamboo and fiberglass rods of comparable quality approximating 3 to 1. This made sense in view of the skill, experience, and hand craftsmanship that went into the construction of a bamboo fly rod as compared with machine-produced synthetic copies. Those who could afford bamboo ably defended their extravagance, noting that a fine bamboo rod has a certain indescribable feel and balance, a sort of "class" if you will, that makes it esthetically pleasing and a delight for precision fly casting. Further, many of the glass rods, including some of the high-priced ones, had thick, fat barrels down at the butt end, giving them a decidedly dead feel, and so the bamboo-versus-fiberglass option was a viable one. I suppose it still is, although in 1974 inflation struck fly fishers, along with everyone else, especially hard. Bamboo rods jumped about 60 percent in price. Money-saving bamboo rod kits were no longer available, and the less-expensive bamboo rods disappeared altogether. Of course, glass-rod prices followed suit, if less dramatically, while new graphite fiber rods made their appearance, selling for unbelievable prices that rivaled those of the previous year's bamboo rods! It's difficult for me to understand how or why mass-produced synthetic fly rods should cost as much as the bamboo variety, but that's how things stand at present. The slender graphites are really quite special. Light in weight, they are inherently rigid and have surprising power for shooting long lines, far more than you would expect on the basis of rod length. There is, however, a negative side too. At least in my experience, a graphite doesn't communicate what it is doing to your hand unless fully extended, and that means throwing a lot of line. There just isn't the familiar feel on short and even medium-range casts; the result is that I lack confidence and lose both accuracy and delicacy. To my way of thinking, the graphite's real value is in long-distance work where this new material has truly provided a tackle "breakthrough."

Unless money isn't an issue, it would seem that you ought to be sure you're really "into" fly fishing before buying a luxury bamboo fly rod, high-priced graphite rod, or even one of the more expensive fiberglass models. A number of companies have rods selling for $50 or less; I really prefer these to the more costly ones. My favorite rod for many seasons was advertised as ideal for a "loaner" or "for that boy who's finally old enough to take along." I can't remember an instance wherein this rod cost me a fish that I might have taken with a fancier weapon. I'll admit that there are unusually demanding situations calling for exquisite fly-casting accuracy and delicacy, but even then, the angler would have to be several cuts above the average in casting skills in order to cash in on his rod's extra quality.

In any event, it is important to emphasize the fact that action, length, and weight individually and collectively have little impact on cost. Fittings such as the reel seat, shaped cork grip, line guides, ferrules, and wrappings can add up to differences of $25 and more. Cheap reel seats bind, ferrules slip or stick, guides flatten or break, and wrappings unravel. However, many of the less expensive rods put out by major manufacturers have reasonably good fittings, and I wouldn't pay a lot to get the top of the line.

Multiple-joint rods, such as the backpacking models, are said to suffer from uneven action due to the numerous rigid ferrule areas. Ferrules are traditionally made of metal, and self ferrules, so-called, formed from the rod blank itself, are currently a hot marketing item. They are supposed to give smoother action than the old type, although I haven't been impressed that this is so at all. Indeed, unlike a metal ferrule, the female part may crack; but in any case, I've used several very satisfactory mulit-joint rods with both kinds of ferrule.

I have little regard for combination spin-fly rods. Spinning rods don't need much character, and the combo rods that I've handled have made poor fly rods, almost without exception. For purposes of two-way fishing, as on a trip to a high lake, I had rather put a spinning reel on a good fly rod. There is very little loss of distance through increased line guide friction.

How many rods does an angler really need? My wife has a strong opinion about this, and I secretly suspect that she is right in that the answer is *one*, although I've somehow acquired an assortment of 14 over the years. In making a selection, remember that the wind has a perfect right to blow at any time, and it usually does. It's just common sense to count on some wind and to come prepared lest you be blasted right out of the water just as I was on the Madison. With this in mind, I would strongly recommend a rod with medium action, not shorter than 7½ feet. Pick one with a reasonably slender barrel that feels good when you wave it around, and I doubt that you'll be disappointed. Among my collection, a nice little 6½ bamboo seldom sees the light of day, because its length, coupled with medium-slow action, makes it inadequate for handling any real breeze, not to mention the other problems that shortness brings to a fly rod.

During the course of an average season, I depend largely on three rods: an eight-footer with action to the slow side of medium for delicate presentations where accuracy is at a premium, another eight-foot rod with an action just to the other side of medium for routine duty, and an 8½-footer with medium to fast action for windy situations requiring extra power. Frankly, the middle rod would cover 95 percent of my needs nicely, although I enjoy having all three, for there are real differences between each of them.

FLY LINES AND REELS

Like fly rods, modern fly lines are probably a bit over-merchandised in the sense that there are now so many types and subtypes, each with a special designation. Not so long ago, if you wanted your line to float, it was necessary to keep the core from getting soaked by dressing the surface with a little grease, otherwise the line became a sinker. Now we have lines specifically designed to float, to sink, and to do both at the same time! The old double taper has been joined by the weight forward line, floating or sinking, and is available in many weights and colors.

Nonetheless, line selection today is actually easier than ever before, thanks to a system for designating *effective line weight*, the most critical factor of all. It's reasonable to assume that most anglers will choose their rod before they worry about a line, and as discussed in the last chapter, the line needs to fit if the rod is to perform as it should. Fast-action rods require a much heavier line to activate them than those with slow action, while medium-action rods generally take a middle-weight line. Traditionally, lines were indirectly graded for weight by means of letter designations that correlated with the diameter of the line. "A" was about the thickest while the "H" caliber corresponded to thin line ends. Of course, the thicker the line, the heavier, but lines with the same diameter letter made from different materials or put out by different companies often had dissimilar weights. Further, tapered lines which are naturally thinnest at the ends, didn't all taper at the same rate, making effective casting weight even more difficult to guess. Modern fly lines come labeled with a nice, clean, single digit that corresponds to the weight of a line segment of defined length. It's not necessary to memorize what the numbers mean, because they are relative. Since even the least-expensive rods have an appropriate line number printed on the barrel, it's just a matter of matching rod and line numbers.

The real beauty of the system lies in the fact that a weight number has the same meaning whether it is attached to a floating line, sinking line, to a floating line with a sinking tip, to a level line, or to any form of tapered line. Of course, the actual load that a rod pulls against in throwing a forward cast is a function of both the intrinsic line weight and the length of line being cast at that particular moment. Manufacturers assign weight numbers based on the effective pull expected during an "average cast."

Thus it follows that a rod calling for an 8-weight line works equally well with a level sinking line or a tapered floater just so long as both are rated as no. 8. It may seem strange that two lines as different as these could have the same effective casting weight, but the designer has several variables to juggle, such as diameter, construction of the core, and the type of surface coating. The density of the core matrix need not be very different in floating and sinking lines. Water has a specific gravity of 1.0 and this defines the break point for floating versus sinking insofar as line density is concerned. A line that weighs in just below this figure tends to float, while one just to the other side will want to sink, and yet their absolute weights could still be pretty similar.

The following chart gives a rough approximation of the way in which line numbers correlate with rod action and length:

LINE NO.	LINE DESCRIPTION	ROD ACTION	ROD LENGTH
3			Short
4	Light	Slow	to
5			Medium
6			
7	Medium	Variable	Variable
8			
9	Heavy	Medium	Medium
10		to Fast	to Long

Middle-weight lines (no. 6, 7, and 8) fit a wide range of rods and are correspondingly the most widely used, since a majority of fly rods have pretty much "middle-of-the-road" action and length. However, there are other rods in which action and length tend to cancel one another. For instance a 6 ½-footer with fast action and a supple nine-footer should both take a middle-weight line.

It isn't absolutely necessary to use a line of the *exact weight* called for; in fact, the average fly caster would have trouble distinguishing between two lines that are one number apart in the first place. Rather, it is the gross mismatch that fouls up your casting.

Thinking back, I was unbelievably naive about this sort of thing in the early days. I particularly remember a disastrous experience on an unusual little creek in Colorado. The rancher who owned this water was a rather eccentric fellow in that he believed all trout fishermen to be mentally deranged, and not wanting a lot of crazy folk running about his property, he generally kept anglers out. Thus the brook was nearly virginal, and by reputation contained more than a few monstrous Browns. I somehow wangled a "one-shot" invitation, and anticipating some fabulous sport, I borrowed a fine old bamboo rod made by the famous Granger Company for the occasion. Suspecting that the big Browns might be less than gullible, despite their sheltered environment, and knowing that the current would be sluggish with areas of shallow water, I planned to use delicate tackle. Since all of my fly lines were heavy, I even purchased a slender double tapered line, without a thought as to its casting weight. It was too late when I discovered that the nine-foot Granger needed a hefty line to flex its springy tip, for I hadn't bothered to test it beforehand. My new tapered line would have been a 3 or 4 weight by today's standards, and so I was no less than four numbers off, and probably five or six! The rancher's plump Jersey cows stopped grazing from time to time that afternoon to watch a "mad" fisherman ranting and raving up and down the brook that ran through their pasture. I couldn't do a thing with this impossible combination until I finally backed way off from the bank and cast some 60 feet into a ponded area. With that much line out, the rod began to respond just a little, but about the time the first huge fish rose to my fly, I also discovered that the field was alive with angry red ants. Indeed, ant hills were as numerous as cow paddies, and I had managed to step into a large hill, the residents of which were up to my waist and climbing fast. Sodden after a hasty trip to the depths of the pond, I climbed into the car, reflecting that the Granger had felt and behaved very much like a broom stick. I was so completely disgusted that when I pulled into the garage, I actually tied the line to a real broom handle, leader, fly, and all. After making sure the neighbors weren't watching, I tried out the rig in the backyard. Sure enough, the broomstick was no worse than the Granger had been for casts up to 30 feet or so!

Remember that the line number is assigned on the basis of an assumption pertaining to the length of an average cast. There is no way to divorce the line's intrinsic weight from cast length when it comes to getting a rod properly cocked, and casts vary from target to target all day long. This brings us to an important point: recommended weights for almost all fly rods seem to be calculated for rather long casts, at least longer ones than I like to make in everyday stream fishing. The shorter your cast, the better, all things considered, and for this reason I frequently use a line that is one number heavier than that suggested for a particular rod. I've repeatedly found that it is better to err on the side of having a little *extra* line weight than not quite enough. This is especially true for those delicate little slack-line casts at close quarters where accuracy is particularly vital. When my line is so short that it barely touches the water, I may even go to one that is two numbers heavier than that recommended for my rod. It's asking a lot of the first ten feet of your line if you expect it to get the rod working decently, let alone to deliver

It often happens that I use the same rod for very different assignments in separate locations. For instance, picture a boulder-strewn river, replete with churning currents and abundant cover. Assume that the rod is an eight-footer with an action on the slow side of medium, rated for a no. 6 line. In this situation, I'll probably use a no. 8 since most of my casts will span only 15 feet or so, and much of that will be covered by the virtually weightless leader. Now the scene (but not the rod) changes to a clear, shallow brook running through open, grassy flats. Skittery Cutthroat are the quarry, and there is hardly any cover; as a result, I find myself firing from 40 feet or more, but this time with a no. 6 line. A difference of 25 feet in average cast length is more than enough to call for a change in lines, and it follows that one rod can do its best for you only if given several lines with which to work.

Floating lines are naturally tools of the dry-fly fisherman, but they aren't his property alone. Bouyant fly lines are also useful in dead drifting sunken flies, because the visible floating end acts as a strike indicator. Floating lines with short sinking tip segments are used with sunken flies too, although they are expensive. I would rather use an old floating line for this purpose, since the worn tip soon gets soaked and sinks nicely on its own.

Sinking lines are supposed to help get a wet fly down, although I generally prefer to weight my flies slightly instead of depending on the line. Sinking lines need time in order to do their job, and in fast water, they must be cast well above the target, a maneuver that just isn't practical on smaller streams or even on rivers at close range. Short casts don't put enough line into the water to sink a fly effectively. Because of its weight, a heavy sinking line is very handy for roll casting a wet fly and can be a terrific help in strong wind. On rare occasions, I have even used a no. 10 sinking line with a relatively small diameter for dry-fly work! Under gale conditions when an ordinary line gets blown right out of the water and flaps like a pennant on a flag pole, this line cuts the wind while the part that's

out of the water is buoyed up sufficiently to prevent the fly from sinking for quite some time.

For reasons best known to the manufacturers, it is costly to build tapers into fly lines, so much so that a double taper or rocket taper will sell for about three times the price of the same brand and quality of level (or untapered) line. Since the better tapered lines run at least $15, the angler who buys one ought to have some sort of advantage over a level-line user. I have checked this out on a number of occasions by alternately fishing with a level and a tapered line matched for casting weight. There's no doubt about it, a tapered line will drop your fly (whether dry or wet) more precisely and gently than one of uniform diameter. Under difficult conditions, this can be a very significant factor, since a level line has a definite tendency to slap down hard and fast, as do the trailing leader and fly.

There are two basic types of tapered lines: the double taper and the weight forward line. Many of them still carry the traditional letter code for diameter as well as the number designation for weight. The popular old HCH double taper weighs in at about a 7 or an 8 in modern lingo. The H at either end indicates a diameter of about .032 inches, tapering gradually to a long central belly segment of C diameter approximating .052 inches. Both ends of the line are of equal quality and have the same taper, and so when one end wears out, it takes its place on the post of the reel spool, and the fresh end is ready—it is really two lines in one. An HEH would correspond to a very light line, and a GAG to a heavy double taper, but today the magic number is what counts most. Weight forward lines (also called shooting or rocket tapers), such as a GAF, are designed for distance casting. The business end has a G diameter that tapers back to a thick, heavy A belly segment some 18 feet from the tip. The belly segment continues back for another 18 feet or so before tapering back down to a level "running line" of F diameter. The idea is to get the heavy belly segment working while the length of line being cast

DRY FLIES, THE WHYS AND WHENS

I don't ordinarily go out of my way to provoke arguments, but on occasion I can't resist getting a rise out of a dry-fly purist, particularly if he's a bit self impressed. It's not hard to do if you begin the conversation with some positive remarks about floating flies, perhaps describing a recent hatch that led to an exciting rise of big trout. When he is properly set up, I drop a word bomb at the end of a sentence, something like this: "and the dry fly is certainly ideal for beginners." It's a good idea to step back out of reach, should the victim react violently, for you will likely have insulted him deeply. You know, though, that it's perfectly true that the road to success is often easiest along the dry-fly route. For one thing, trout rise readily to surface food, they really like to feed on top and often do so preferentially. You may have read that trout take only a small amount of their diet from the surface; I've seen estimates as low as 5 to 10 percent for Brooks and Rainbows, with Browns rated at 15 to 20 percent in this regard. These studies were carefully done on stomach contents, and while I have no wish to quarrel with them, I wouldn't be too impressed either. In the first place, the best dry-fly fishing takes place during the warm months when the trout are taking most of their surface food, and so overall low percentages are misleading. Secondly, there is a fundamental difference between where fish actually *get* their food and where they are *willing* to take it. In other words, perhaps the trout in a certain stream do take only 20 percent of their diet off the top, but how do we know they wouldn't be happy to make this figure 90 percent if the right insects presented themselves often enough and in adequate numbers?

There are other very good reasons for the floating fly's popularity, all of them hinging on visibility. Frankly, I suspect that many of us enjoy just watching the fly bob along, even as children enjoy floating paper boats down a rain-filled gutter. There is nothing quite like the excitement that comes when a trout suddenly appears on a collision course with your fly, takes it, and reacts to the unexpected sting of the hook. In fact, there is a certain sense of pregnant anticipation even before you see the fish, as if the innocent fly were a sacrificial animal staked out to lure a marauding tiger. (This comparison is not overly dramatic when you think what the gaping, tooth-jammed jaws of a trout must look like from an insect's vantage point!) As a more practical consideration, it's usually easy to see rises to a floating fly in the interests of setting the hook, an advantage that's often denied the wet-fly fisherman. Thus, in the ongoing and ancient debate between dry- and wet-fly advocates, the principal planks in the dry-fly supporter's platform include the following:

1. Trout feed readily on the surface.
2. Surface strikes are exciting.
3. Setting the hook is easier if the fly is visible.

It may be a left-handed sort of compliment, but I really feel that a dry fly is the logical approach for new fly fishermen. It offers plenty of visual kicks to hold their interest, while technical requirements are reduced to a relative minimum.

Traditionally, the dry fly devotee is a nicely garbed gentleman, sporting a deerstalker cap. He should puff on his vintage briar while wielding a fine rod over exclusive club waters. In short, he's an angler with considerable "class." It would appear that this image has become a bit tarnished, at least it has for me. In my mind's eye, I tend to see instead a somewhat wet and muddy 12-year-old clad in tee shirt and jeans. He's playing a fish and blowing bubble gum bubbles, all at the same time, a trick I'll bet few sophisticates could manage! When conditions are right, dry-fly fishing can become a veritable cinch. Two students put on a convincing demonstration to this effect recently when we tackled a river that runs through a deep gorge along the Colorado-New Mexico line. One fellow was an experienced bait and lure fisherman who hadn't tried flies before, and the other's total exposure was limited to a little lawn casting. As it turned out, each of them caught about as many trout as I did, despite all the hours of "dry flying" time I had logged in the past. I didn't spend a lot of time coaching them either, for I was engrossed with an experiment of my own and actually fished fairly intently. This particular water was hard to get at, and consequently it contained an abundance of eager trout. Further, the river bed was littered with boulders and down timber that created considerable coarse detail. Thus the water was very easy to read and angler cover was plentiful. Our approaches were close, casts were simple, and rises were obvious. I had seen to it that their tackle was adequate, and so after a few hours, they got along nicely on their own. Of course, things aren't always so easy, but the excellent results enjoyed by my novice friends make a point, I think.

As you might guess, floating flies aren't necessarily magical, and trout response to them varies. How, then, do you recognize conditions that suggest potential success with dry flies? This is a more complicated matter than most beginners realize, for there are certain misconceptions that can hold back a learner's progress severely.

Concept: Dry flies are apt to produce only when the fish are actively feeding on the surface. Reality: Nothing could be further from the truth; an absence of feeding activity means little, although dry-fly fishermen are naturally glad to see spontaneous rises.

Concept: Surface rises indicate that dry-fly fishing will be good. Reality: Unfortunately not. At times, trout rising to a hatch are unbelievably critical of artificial flies, practically finning their noses at one pattern after another.

Concept: When a hatch is in progress, the artificial must copy the natural exactly if it is to be successful. Reality: Sometimes yes, many times no. Individual streams vary a lot in this regard.

Concept: One fly pattern is just about as good as any other as long as its size is right. Reality: It all depends on the time and place.

Concept: Good dry-fly water is low and clear. Reality: This is another tradition that trout don't always follow. Superb surface fishing sometimes develops in the face of high, discolored water if conditions aren't extreme. A little roil helps hide the angler while lulling the trout into a false sense of security. "Poor" dry-fly water can produce the easiest fishing of all. (Water temperature is a variable that's worth measuring, for with readings below about 45 degrees, I have seldom seen significant surface feeding. Apart from numbing the trout into torpid inactivity, frigid water discourages most insects from hatching in the first place, and so there is little natural incentive for the trout to rise.)

Concept: Good dry-fly weather is warm, clear, and windless. Reality: Don't bet on it, trout will rise in a snowstorm and I've benefited on many occasions from gusty winds that blew a smorgasbord of insects from bankside brush into the water, causing generalized feeding excitement.

Thus, there are no absolute ways to determine if dry flies will or won't be effective, at least not with any degree of certainty. For this reason, I recommend occasional brief dry-fly trials during the day, utilizing several patterns and several hook sizes. A half-hour should be long enough to derive some sort of indication, whether positive or negative. There is just no substitute for an actual test, no matter how bleak the prospects may seem. For instance, there are those occasions when a small number of highly prized naturals begin to hatch, perhaps without becoming conspicuous themselves or creating an obvious rise. This event may very well trigger widespread interest in surface food of any type, precisely the situation that one hopes to reveal by means of a dry-fly trial!

One October, several of us planned to fish the spectacular Rio Grande Gorge in northern New Mexico, the "Box" as it is fondly known, in hopes that a warm, dry fall had brought favorable water conditions. However, as luck would have it, an early season blizzard coincided neatly with the first day of our trip, turning the Rio Grande into a great, green torrent. Instead of fishing, we spent the afternoon watching fluffy snowflakes fill the Taos Plaza from the drugstore window, between innings of the World Series. Things looked better the next morning under a sparkling sun, and so we headed for the more accessible Red River where it enters a rugged box canyon of its own on the way to the Rio Grande a few miles to the west. The Red River was beginning to roil too, although it registered a relatively balmy 54 degrees in comparison with the distinctly chilly air temperature of 38 degrees. Bright green conifers and jagged black lava cliffs, powdered with snow, stood out starkly against a vivid blue sky as we skidded down a snow-buried trail into the canyon. The day grew pleasantly warm, but this brought snowmelt from the high Sangre de Cristo Range above, causing the river to chill, rise, and discolor. We had only modest success with a variety of wet flies until toward 2:00 p.m., when my fishing partner announced that he was switching to floaters! I shook my head in mock disbelief. This was surely a foolish move in view of the degenerating water conditions, but as he put it, "if I can't catch fish, I'd rather do it with dry flies." Surprisingly, when I glanced up a few minutes later he was holding a nice Brown, and when he hooked a second in the next pocket, I knew it was I who had missed something. Sure enough, when I looked really carefully a few small May fly duns were coming off the water. Thanks to my restless friend, the remainder of that afternoon was much more productive, and I might add that dry flies earned a big edge over the bait and lures offered by our competitors. Parenthetically, this experience brings to mind the fact that Browns are apparently attracted to flies more than to bait and lures. To my knowledge, this very heavily fished portion of the Red River is stocked only with Rainbow, and yet most of our trout were Brownies taken from within two miles of the main parking area for fishermen. In other words, we were probably taking fish that had refused untold numbers of baited hooks and lures during the previous summer. This sort of preferential catch of Browns on flies in streams with mixed trout populations is a fairly common occurrence. Browns get a high priority from fly fishers, perhaps not because they take flies better than other trout, but because they hit bait and lures less eagerly than their finny friends of other species.

While the Red River fooled me with a combination of bad water and nice weather, the opposite mix of "anti-dry fly" circumstances nearly defeated me one September in Yellowstone. Although the day dawned with a high overcast, I had no serious weather worries as I waded into the lower end of the Firehole River canyon. I'd just released my second smallish trout when dense shrouds of grey mist appeared above, obliterating the high cliffs and rolling rapidly downriver. Only minutes later, a steady gale was upon me, and with it came a fine rain, driven almost parallel to the surface. I was soaked through so quickly that my raincoat became a useless afterthought, and retreating to the car, I watched the storm slowly worsen over the next half-hour. Then it occurred to me that since the wind was blowing from one direction, I might be able to escape by finding a meandering stream whose twisting channel would allow me to cast with the wind rather than into its teeth. The nearby Gibbon River looked ideal, and my hopes picked up when I found this sinuously picturesque trout stream running clear and in the mid-50s. By then the rain had turned to sleet, but after all, I rationalized, the miserable conditions are all above water, and it may be a fairly nice day for the trout. This was indeed wishful thinking. Virtually my entire collection of nymphs and streamers, fished in every way I knew, failed to bring so much as the hint of a strike. At noon, I huddled behind the trunk of a lonely tree with a sandwich, for it was snowing fitfully, and the temperature had fallen some 20 degrees. Aside from the vapor plumes of far-off geysers, the only life I had seen was provided by a few fluttering Caddis flies in the tall grass along the bank. Which was it to be, a hot shower back at the motel, or another try? Reluctantly, I decided to go with a dry fly, not so much with any real expectation of success, as with the hope of false casting up some body heat in order to beat the chill factor for a little longer.

The beige-colored Caddis were big fellows, fluttering moth-like from frond to frond of snow-plumed grass that fringed the still water, and although I hadn't seen a rise, the flies did occasionally touch the surface for an instant. I tied on a matching no. 12 Ginger Quill with numb, clumsy fingers, casting it straight up the bank edge onto overhanging grass stems. I gently twitched the fly into the water, inches from the bank, and after a few seconds of dead drift, I again twitched the Ginger Quill, ever so slightly, with the rod tip so that it fluttered, Caddis-style. The flakes were falling quite fast when I saw a dark swirl beneath the fly; a repeat presentation brought the first strike I'd seen in hours. After that it didn't seem cold at all! Although only an occasional cast brought a rise, the Yellowstone Cutthroat were generally good sized and remarkably lively. It was enormously satisfying to escape the skunking for which I had been so surely headed, frostbite notwithstanding! These Caddis not only tipped me off as to the kind of fly I needed, but also as to the size and color, since the fish were apparently selective in this regard. Beyond this, the naturals even told me precisely *where* to put my fly because interestingly enough, I got no strikes more than six inches or so from the water's edge.

As on the Red and Gibbon Rivers, naturals sometimes point the way to potential surface action when there are no rises to be seen. You just can't expect insects to appear in quantities such that the sky darkens with their numbers! Remember, too, that rises from sizable trout may only dimple the surface or may be hidden by flecks of foam or glare, hence the wisdom of a dry-fly trial.

It would appear that there are about as many dry-fly patterns as there are stars in the sky, and here we have the makings of a real dilemma since an angler can generally display only one pattern at a time. My collection of dry flies started out naturally enough with those that were popular in the Denver area where I grew up, a managable group of eight or so patterns. Then I read Ray Bergman's classic book, *Trout*, with its fine accounts of fishing in New York and environs. Fascinated by the colored fly plates, I saved enough money for a fairly complete selection of basically eastern patterns. Now Tup's Indispensibles, Quill Gordons, and Hendrickson's joined the western Mosquito, Cow Dung, and Rio Grande King in my expanding fly boxes. Later, Ernie Schwiebert's excellent book, *Matching the Hatch*, came along, a beautifully written and illustrated piece that correlates the actual insects upon which trout feed with specific matching patterns. Up to this point, I had chosen patterns because of their reputations or pleasing appearance, picking the fly I would use on a hunch basis, very much like someone playing the horses. I was highly impressed by the concept of hatch matching because Schwiebert put some science and logic into the often mysterious feeding antics of trout. He explained that May flies are the most important insects on many streams, prevalent throughout the season in one species or another, and enjoying lobster or roast beef status on the trout's menu. As described earlier, many May fly species hatch from the aquatic nymph form by shedding their final nymph skin in the surface film. This is a hazardous time for them because they can't fly to safety as yet and are essentially sitting ducks for the waiting trout, the perfect setup for a dry fly. If he survives, the young adult is known as a *dun* because of dull coloration and opaque wings. A final molt soon after in streamside brush produces the sexually mature *spinner*, a brighter insect with shiny, transparent wings. Spinners, too, may cause a rise when they fall into the water during the process of mating, laying eggs, or later, in the throes of death. Of course after reading Schwiebert, I had to have matching patterns for all of the western species, duns and spinners, males and females. This amounted to an addition of about 30 patterns, but he also described Caddis and Stone flies—could they be ignored? Schwiebert pointed out that Caddis hatch from free-swimming pupal forms, and although not necessarily so concentrated, their hatches can also cause a heavy rise. I learned that Stone fly nymphs shuck their skins by crawling out of the water onto rocks and are less vulnerable during the hatching process. However, the rather clumsy adults like to frolic about in wave-tossed, fast water and can be most interesting to the trout. If I were to become a devoted hatch matcher, I would need another 15 Caddis and Stone fly patterns, and so it went. Multiplying fly boxes bulged my pockets as I clattered and clanked along. It was no easy matter to remember which pocket held which fly from a menagerie that had reached an impressive total of 73 patterns! I needed a portable filing system, and terrible frustrations befell me when I realized that I could only fish with a small fraction of my flies at any one time (1/73rd to be exact). It got to a point where I frequently spent more time changing patterns than fishing, and it took days to catalog the whole mess. One fall, when the season was about over, I decided to see which patterns had been most effective. To my chagrin, only 31 of the 73 had even been called into action that year. Of these, 26 had taken at least one trout, but only eight had logged enough fishing time for a fair evaluation. Like a stamp or coin hobbyist, I had become more of a collector than a user. About this time I got around to reading John Atherton's book, *The Fish and the Fly*. Atherton believed that an artificial fly needn't match the natural exactly in order to be successful, so long as its appearance *suggested* the insect or gave an *impression* of it. His impressionistic patterns were tied with mixtures of materials chosen for color, texture, and sheen. Atherton copied the size of a natural carefully but made no attempt to slavishly mimic precise colors or form. It was the difference between an impressionistic painting and a photographically sharp reproduction of the same scene or object. It was an arty concept perhaps, but Atherton was a professional artist as well as an expert angler. The real beauty of impressionistic flies was that a single pattern served as a "match" for not just one, but a number of natural insects. I was most impressed to learn that Atherton got along splendidly with a half-dozen or so patterns from one end of the season to the other, and on difficult eastern waters at that! It seemed obvious that it was high time to being a housecleaning of my museum, but where to begin? I started by eliminating certain look-alike patterns, although it was painful to shelve old favorites, and this still left me with about fifty. Then I took a hard look at records from the past five seasons, focusing on matching patterns in particular. In retrospect, I had accomplished remarkably little in a practical sense despite a sincere interest in streamside entomology. Surely I had learned to recognize the sail plane glide of the May fly in contrast to the darting flutter of Caddis and Stone flies. I could even identify the more common species of slender-bodied May flies with their delicate legs, wispy tails, and upright wings. I now knew that both Caddis and Stone flies folded their wings backward, tent-like, and that the Caddis were covered with fine hairs, while the Stonies were distinguished by an extra pair of wings. Even though I felt much more knowledgeable, I wondered how many successes had been based on insect identification and how many entomological coups I had pulled off. In the first place, during a span of more than 100 consecutive fishing days spent in five western states, there really hadn't been very many hatches to match! Most of the hatches I had recorded were either skimpy or brief, anyway, leaving the balance of the day "hatchless." Even more disappointing was the fact that when a hatch did come along, the trout had usually proven to be less than properly selective. This bothered me because it seemed that if one went to all the trouble of carefully matching the naturals, the trout should at least demand the "correct" pattern and not just rise to any old pattern, as they so often did. Still, there had been scattered instances when the trout were exquisitely selective, so much so that I couldn't take them with any of my patterns, including the special matching ones. I became an advocate of impressionism, therefore, although without turning entirely from the matching patterns either.

The idea of capturing natural insects for purposes of achieving an exact match is pleasingly logical, although not always too practical. Some species swarm all over you during a hatch and are easily examined, but others are either more coy or come off water that's hard to reach. It may boil down to deciding between your fly rod and a butterfly net. It isn't hard to guess the size of naturals in flight, but color is another matter, even at close range. As a rule, size is usually the more important feature in terms of selecting an effective artificial, and so when it comes down to deciding between fishing and fly chasing, I keep right on pitching patterns unless the naturals are easy to grab. This is a less than scientific approach, but hatches may last for only a few minutes, and time really races by when the big ones are coming up!

I do about 80 percent of my dry-fly work with one or another of a small group of impressionistic patterns. The Adams is an excellent example, employing a life-like mixture of two hackles, brown and grizzly (finely banded black and white feathers from a Plymouth Rock rooster). Real insects don't come with two-tone wings and legs, but there is impressionistic magic in this particular blend, at least in the trout's eyes, for the Adams is a great favorite nation-wide. Its blue-grey fur-dubbed body is lustrous and slightly translucent. The wings are grizzly hackle tips, and the tail is composed of the same feather blend as the hackle. Atherton liked shiny furs and feathers in patterns like this, and

commonplace for them—almost trite, I suppose. The Royal may attract scorn from some fishermen, but rarely from the trout, and with me, results come before prestige!

An artificial has four pieces of anatomy, hackle, wings, body, and tail. To my way of thinking, a dry fly's soul is in its hackle, the other components are of secondary importance, with certain special exceptions. This is a traditional viewpoint; however, there is a lot of current interest in hackleless dry flies that lie flat in the surface film, presenting their bodies and outstretched wings for inspection. Many of my friends have not been particularly impressed with the no-hackle creations because they float so poorly in rough water. The hackle has several purposes. It represents the legs, antennae, and, to an extent, the wings of the insect. At the same time, it holds the body and part of the hook up above the surface film, presumably making them less clearly visible to the trout. The whole plan is to create a blurred, nebulous image that *suggests* the natural insect. I believe that there is a place for hackleless flies under certain difficult conditions as in copying spent spinners on glassy surfaces, but for most fishing, there is nothing wrong with the old standard dry fly. It's interesting that the famous Spider dry flies, earlier and still popular eastern favorites, are tied with very long hackle feathers and no wings or significant body! It seems that fishermen have a hard time making up their minds.

Most naturals are basically brown or sometimes he added a bit of tinsel ribbing to the bodies of his flies with the idea of reflecting glints of light, copying the surfaces of natural insects. Perhaps the renowned Royal Coachman owes its effectiveness to contrasting yet peculiarly impressionistic mixtures of white (wings), brown (hackle), and red/green (silk and peacock herl body). The Royal is anything but a hatch matcher. Nonetheless, its fame is based on a record of remarkable productivity rather than its flashy appearance or catchy name. I've met sophisticated fishermen who wouldn't use or admit to using this pattern; it's too showy and grey, comprising a spectrum of shades from very dark (virtually black) to pale gingers or pearl greys. Brown flies may have a yellow, reddish or pink cast, while the greys commonly show bluish overtones. Hackles come in all of these shades and colors and may be mixed, as in the Adams. Wings are tied in different forms and colors or may be left out altogether. Potential body constructions are even more complex, not to mention a variety of tail materials. If we start to list all of the variables involved in each of the four parts of a fly's anatomy, and think of the possible permutations and combinations, pattern construction becomes a staggering proposition.

It is possible to predict the degree of selectiveness the trout in a given stream are likely to show because intrinsically food-rich waters support fish that tend to be much more critical than those from "poor neighborhoods." Take a relatively low altitude stream with clean, well-oxygenated water suitable for trout, possibly a winding meadow brook flanked by buggy, overhanging banks. Throw in beds of water weed that support tiny shrimp and other prime fodder, and you have a lushly provident setting that will likely produce impressive hatches, together with large and highly selective trout. Living in the midst of plenty, these finny gourmets are likely to try the patience of the most skillful and compulsive hatch matcher. To add to the angler's woes, these fish have little need to forage around for food between hatches. Compare this stream with one just below timberline, fed by melt from snowbanks and rushing swiftly

over a bottom of polished rock. Here summer is short, water temperatures are always chill, there is little moss, and currents are too rapid for many insect species. I can't recall a single instance wherein the trout were particularly critical in this kind of setting. Indeed, they are usually glad to see almost any fly, water temperatures permitting. Of course, many streams fall somewhere in between the rich and poor extremes for food content, but in my experience the really finicky fish that demand meticulous copies of the naturals have come from justifiably famous trout waters, the truly great American fly streams. Unfortunately, these are hardly everyday fishing holes for most of us, and while I have several boxes of specific matching patterns for such special spots, I no longer carry them routinely. There is a practical limit to the number of flies one can lug around, and having a huge traveling collection is no guarantee that you will have exactly what selective trout demand anyway. Minor modifications of special matching patterns are often necessary to satisfy them, and it's sometimes amazing how much difference a tiny change can make.

The Adams and Royal Coachman are solid keystones in any fly collection, and in addition, I would suggest a fly with blue dun (grey-blue) hackle such as the Grey Wulff. The buggy Wulff series of dry flies is distinguished by bushy wings and tails tied with hair. This construction makes them very buoyant for rough water floating and more visible too. The Irresistibles are another dry-fly series built with fat bodies of clipped, shaped, deer hair to obtain good floatation as well as impressionism. These flies are nearly as buoyant as cork, and their rotund bodies suggest the silhouette of a floating beetle or grasshopper. In this case, body shape and floatation quality seem to be far more important than hackles or coloration. Irresistibles are good flies for beginners, although certain crafty Idaho friends take huge Rainbows with them from challenging Silver Creek, sometimes in the midst of a select hatch!

Thus, different parts of a fly may be

designed for special purposes. The Royal's white wing improves visibility for angler and trout alike; hair wings, body, and tail help with floatation or create a life-like silhouette, and so on. If we go very far into the matter of individual patterns, the lid to Pandora's box will open wide, so I would rather summarize the principles behind an effective dry-fly collection as follows:

First, develop favorite patterns of your own, patterns in which you have *confidence*. I could list my own, but they wouldn't necessarily be any better than others. An angler should *believe* that his fly will do its job if presented properly, as if he and the fly were members of a team. Thus he is free to concentrate on critical tasks such as water reading, casting, watching for strikes, etc. If one has the dispiriting feeling that his fly has poor credibility with the fish, attention naturally wanders, and angler performance suffers.

Secondly, hold down the number of patterns you carry to a reasonable total. There is more to be lost than gained by playing pattern roulette; many accomplished fishermen carry no more than a half-dozen. I'd shoot for variation in hackle color within this select group, rather than worrying primarily about wings and bodies.

Third, stock plenty of hook sizes, for, as a general rule, size is at least as important as pattern. I would far rather carry a few dependable patterns in a wide range of sizes than vice versa. Dry flies lead dangerous lives. Leaders snap, hook points and barbs break, and even the best tied flies eventually succumb to hard use. It's tough to hook a good trout and lose your fly in the process, only to find that it was your only fly in that pattern and size. On the water, I carry up to six flies in one pattern and size depending on expected needs. Anglers who use a smaller number of patterns can carry (and afford) more flies in each size, too.

DRY-FLY SIZE

There are sharp differences of opinion among fishermen about fly size. Just what is a "large fly," and what does "small" really mean in terms of hook caliber? These questions provide more ammunition for arguments than you might think. It would be interesting to give a random group of anglers a questionnaire in which they are asked to match hook caliber against a prepared list of adjective descriptions by filling in the blanks:

HOOK CALIBER

Too Large! .... _____
Largest Commonly Used ..... _____
Favorite Hook Size .... _____
Smallest Commonly Used ..... _____
Too Small! .... _____

According to my observations, two opinionated groups should emerge from this study. One would show a bias for larger hooks, generally regarding a no. 18 fly as "too small" and putting no. 12s in the medium range. Then there would be another polarized group of midget-fly fans who feel that no. 14s are "too large," while rating no. 28s as merely "small." (There really are such hooks.) For them there's no such thing as a hook that's too small. Indeed, nature makes her flies in sizes ranging from no. 8s (or even larger in the case of certain Stone fly species) to the nearly microscopic no. 28s, so neither group is exactly off base. However, there is a place for flexibility, common sense, and moderation, as in any set of options. While my questionnaire idea is admittedly fanciful, each of us does in fact impose limits as to the largest and smallest flies we like to fish with.

There are several situations in which the plumper patterns have been quite useful. These big "sofa pillows," as they are called, are popular on broad-chested, brawling rivers such as the Madison. They can entice a big Rainbow to come busting up from his holding pocket through the tough current, probably thinking the reward will be a huge natural or perhaps a fat grasshopper. These large artificials are often productive wherever grasshoppers abound, and I also use them when visibility is limited by gathering darkness or murky water, as in the early season. However, during an average year, I take relatively few trout on no. 8s and no. 10s. The no. 12 is a transition caliber, leading to the versatile no. 14 hook. If a poll of dry-fly fishers were actually taken, I'd bet on the 14 to win the vote for most popular hook size. It is neither very large nor very small, and a no. 14 artificial approximates many natural insects as they appear on the water. Consequently, it's easy to find no. 14s behind tackle counters in a number of patterns.

Let's take a look at the no. 16s and no. 18s, sizes that many consider too small to be useful. Why? For one thing, smaller flies are harder to follow on the water, and this can surely be a liability at times. Secondly, since hook caliber is determined by the gap or distance between the point and the shaft, small hooks take a thinner bite of tissue from the trout's lip, tongue, or jaw and can tear out more easily than their larger counterparts. The fine wire from which delicate hooks are necessarily made sometimes straightens or breaks, just as the finer tippets that should be used with small flies are prone to snap if they are abused. Petite sizes are harder to find in stock, and from the 16s on down, may be more costly. The biggest deterrent of all is psychological. At first glance, small flies don't look as if they could really capture a trout. I find it very difficult to convince a beginner that no. 18s are good for anything beyond decorative tie clasps. However, on the positive side of the ledger, there are two facts that deserve our fullest attention:

1. Small naturals are extremely prevalent and trout are very fond of them, size notwithstanding. (As already established, effective hatch matching must begin with fly size.)

2. For reasons best known to the trout, they often find smaller flies more believa-

ble than the "sofa pillows" and rise to them with special enthusiasm.

These are highly practical considerations that can influence an angler's catch in an immediate and direct way.

Going a step further, there is no correlation whatever between the caliber of your fly and the size of the fish it will catch. Old, suspicious trout sometimes fall prey to a seductively petite creation, having refused countless flies of a grosser sort over the seasons.

I have studied the influence of hook caliber many times by fishing one size against another in the same pattern on appropriate tippets. I usually being with a no. 16, switch to a 12, then to an 18 and finally to a 14, fishing with each for exactly 30 minutes. In order to account for time lost while changing position, playing a trout, preening the fly back into shape, freeing up a snag and the like, I use a stopwatch so that only actual fishing time is charged against each hook caliber. I then record the number of strikes and number of fish hooked for each hook size during its stint. Obviously, results aren't always the same, but there has been a consistent pattern. I've found that hook caliber seldom influences the absolute number of strikes obtained during the trial period to any great extent, but when it comes to the number of trout *hooked*, the 16s and 18s often enjoy an edge of as much as 3 to 1 over the larger sizes. The percentage of trout that I am able to *land* may be slightly lower for the 18s, although not enough to offset the advantage in the total number hooked, so the final catch total also favors the smaller sizes. The no. 12 finishes last more often than any other caliber unless the water is a bit high or discolored.

Those of us who are privileged to live close enough to a trout stream that we can fish it throughout the season have an opportunity to learn special tricks by comparing conditions and requirements at one time with those prevalent at another. A meandering brook in the high prairies of Colorado's South Park literally forced us to run through a whole gamut of hook sizes during the year, and even during the course of a single day! Repeated trials during late May and early June showed that the trout rose to a no. 10 or a 12 better than to smaller flies. The discolored water was still high with relatively little natural surface food available, and the trout seemed excited by robust, highly visible artificials. By August, 75 percent of the stream's volume had disappeared, draining eastward toward the thirsty plains. Beginning at about 10 a.m., I was usually able to score well with a no. 14 in low, clear water. By noon, however, rises became feeble and furtive. At this point, I discovered that I could greatly improve the situation by simply stepping down to a no. 16, at least until about 2:00 p.m., when this size too became ineffective. Sure enough, an 18 would then re-establish credibility, although the hot sun of later afternoon usually found me plying the water with a 20 or a 22. So, surprisingly enough, fishing stayed good all day if you had the right fly size. Were there various hatches to account for this phenomenon? Not that I could tell. The brook wasn't terribly rich in insect life, and pattern seemed to make relatively little difference! As you can see, those of us who knew the "sliding size" trick had quite an advantage.

Small hooks have some other things going for them. They are remarkably good floaters, thanks to their light weight and also to the reduced bulk of water-absorbent tying materials that go into the construction of tiny flies. They are also sharper, because thinner hook points penetrate tough mouth parts more easily than those of heavy gauge hooks. As to breaking or straightening, there should be no serious problem, since the high quality steel in smaller caliber hooks is pretty tough if handled properly. A significant plus is the fact that small hooks can be removed almost as harmlessly as the barbless kind if you wish to release your trout (a practice we all should follow).

If no. 18 flies are so devastating, what about even smaller ones? I began by listing certain negative features that inevitably accompany the use of delicate hooks, and with the exception of the psychological aspect, they are generally valid. It seems that

66

as hook caliber diminishes beyond a no. 18, these minus factors become increasingly bothersome until at some point, ultra-small hooks are a liability. This point is not always easy to define except by trial and error, but unless you are getting a payoff in better results, I see no reason to use a fly that is smaller than necessary. There are better ways to impress your friends. On the other hand, I definitely feel that the 16s and 18s should become regular members of your fly team. For what it's worth, I've listed the approximate percentage of an average season's dry-fly catch by hook size in my own fishing:

HOOK CALIBER	% OF CATCH
10 ⎱ ⎰ 12	10
14	35
16	40
18	15

This chart suggests that I neglect midges, that is, sizes 20 and smaller. This isn't so at all, for at times they are essential. These little fellows are usually tied without wings, and rather than conforming to specific patterns, tend to feature a basic color in body and hackle. I carry black, grey (grizzly), blue dun, ginger, and brown mixed with grizzly hackled midges. It would appear that precise pattern selectivity falls off as hook size diminishes beyond the no. 18.

True sized hackles are those traditionally considered to be normal for a particular gauge hook in terms of fiber length. This means that the tips of the hackle feathers fan out from the shaft of the hook about half again the distance between the point and the shaft. For reasons to be discussed in the chapter on fly tying, hackle is sometimes tied into a fly which is either longer or shorter than normal for that hook. The point is that hackle length influences the apparent (and actual) size of a fly more than does hook caliber. Thus if a no. 18 hook is fitted with a no. 16 hackle, the fly essentially becomes a 16. This is fine if, for some reason, you want a small hooked no. 16 fly. However, if a true no. 18 is what you're after, as is usually the case, better buy or tie one with normal hackle. There is a tendency for commercial tiers to overhackle many of their smaller flies, and I would keep this in mind when picking out an assortment.

LARGER HOOK WITH "NORMAL" HACKLE MAKES SMALLER FLY . . . THAN . . .

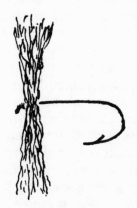

SMALL HOOK WITH "LONG" HACKLE

THE STRIKE/HOOK RATIO

It seems to me that early experiences along the stream are the best remembered, particularly those that teach a lesson. In this regard, I recall (with painful clarity) an afternoon on the Little Snake River in northwestern Colorado during my first year of dry-fly fishing. The events are indelibly etched, for this was by far the most exciting angling I had enjoyed up to that time, and on this occasion, I learned that just as barking dogs don't bite, rising trout don't necessarily, either! Indeed, my artificial attracted no less than 113 distinct strikes in a period of about two hours, and yet I caught only three smallish trout! Of course, sane people don't try to count the number of strikes they get, but my anger and frustration were such that I actually began to keep a tally. How could so many fish hit my fly and get away scot free? These were very evident, splashy strikes too, featuring a violent attack upon the fly followed by a frenzied retreat. If these ambivalent fish were interested enough to go to the trouble of striking, why the sudden change in attitude at "impact"? Or were they insincere throughout the attack and retreat parts of the strike sequence, as if on a playful scouting mission? When I began to study each rise intently, I found that the fish were really just "molesting" the fly rather than actually biting it. Some of the finny acrobats jumped nimbly over my floater without making contact, Jack and the candlestick fashion. Others bumped it from below with their snouts or lashed it with their tails by turning broadside at the last instant. A few seemed to take a gingerly nip, but were gone long before I could strike back. These trying trout reminded me of someone gingerly testing an electric iron with wetted finger to see if it's ready to use. It was probably no accident that two of the three "hot iron" trout I hooked had my fly embedded in their flanks. Mercifully, they finally stopped rising, for my nerves were about shot, and standing by the now-quiet pool, I reflected upon the stunning discrepancy between the amount of action I had experienced and an empty creel. In fact, the number of strikes compared with the number of fish hooked added up to a ratio of 38 to 1!

I've since found that the strike/hook ratio can be an accurate means of evaluating a particular fly's credibility rating with the trout. The point is that trout rise to artificial flies in a variety of ways. On the one hand, they may take deeply and surely, literally swallowing the steel and feathers before leisurely swimming off to enjoy their supposed prize. In this circumstance, the angler has several seconds in which to set his hook, and while a strike/hook ratio of 1 to 1 is impossible in the long run, one can come pretty close. For instance, 20 strikes and 16 hooked (yielding a ratio of 1.25 to 1) is not at all unrealistic. On other occasions, when the fish are side-swiping or just mouthing the fly, ratios naturally soar. Hot-iron strikes generally mean trouble, because most of the trout in a given setting usually react in pretty much the same way to a single pattern and size. In other words, it's uncommon to find very many slow confident risers mixed in with the skittish kind. Implicit in all this is the idea that the angler may be able to do something that will turn a high ratio in a downward direction, and his luck in an upward direction.

If the observed ratio is 2 to 1 or less, leave well enough alone, your fly has reasonably good credibility. Otherwise, consider one or several of the following suggestions.

1. Change to a hook one size smaller in the same pattern you've been using. It makes no difference what the original size was, drop down one caliber. I've often seen ratios of 6 to 1 or higher cut to less than half by simply dropping one hook caliber, a no. 12 to a no. 14, a 14 to a 16, or whatever. And, if a single jump is helpful, a double jump may be more productive still; it's worth a try! This concept was introduced

in the preceding chapter, but remember that changing your fly size is likely to influence the number of strikes you get less than the number of trout hooked, hence a lowered strike/hook ratio means an improved catch.

2. Change to a finer tippet. Of course, this change goes along with a smaller fly, the plan being to obtain a more natural float via a thinner, more flexible tippet. Thus, if your no. 12 fly was tied on 2X, try a 14 on 3X or even 4X if the bulk of the fly and the wind conditions permit.

3. Switch to a new pattern. Assuming that there is no hatch to match, I usually try fairly major changes at first, as from a dark to a light fly, from a basically brown pattern to a blue dun or grey one, and so on. There are certainly occasions when pattern dominates hook size in setting the strike/hook ratio. One afternoon not long ago, we enjoyed some fine dry-fly fishing on Colorado's scenic Crystal River despite the absence of a hatch. Fat Rainbows came up nicely to a variety of patterns in sizes 12 through 18, showing only a slight preference for no. 14s. Just for fun, I made it a rule to change patterns every twenty minutes, meanwhile recording strike/hook ratios. By evening, I had obtained data on nine patterns with ratios varying from less than 2 to 1 all the way up to 8 to 1. Seven flies showed ratios of 4 to 1 or higher, while the Adams turned in a commendable record of 21 rises and 13 hooked. I retested the Adams midway through the afternoon and again just before quitting with about the same ratio each time. Interestingly, no single pattern drew fewer than five strikes during its twenty minutes, nor more than eight.

4. Change to a fresh fly, not necessarily in a different pattern or size, but to a new, crisp, high-floating fly. Hackleless dry flies notwithstanding, I would always bet on a nicely floating imitation over a sodden, half-submerged fly, and this preference is not necessarily restricted to sophisticated fish. While they don't provide very glamourous fishing, you can learn a lot from friendly little Brook trout. One day I stopped by a high meadow creek in Colora-

do's Gore Range to try out some experimental dry-fly patterns on its usually ravenous Brookies. Pattern number one got off to an excellent start, taking four of the first five trout that rose to it inside of 10 minutes. I carefully preened the fly back into floating condition after each release, but only one of the next six risers was hooked. I assumed that a hatch was about to begin, accounting for the fly's sudden loss of popularity. However, no naturals appeared nor were there rise rings to be seen. Soon the ratio reached 15 to 1, and so I changed to a second pattern. To my surprise, this very different fly was as hot as the first one had been, at least in the beginning when it floated nicely. Again, the strike/hook ratio progressively worsened, and it quickly became evident that pattern made no difference whatever as long as the fly floated up on its hackle tips! You'll find that a combination of fish slime, blood, and water will eventually soak up the best tied dry fly so that it no longer floats well, no matter how carefully cleaned and dried. Don't wait for this to happen; if naive little Brookies care about the way your fly floats, so should you! I carry a strip of absorbent cloth pinned to the inside of my jacket for blotting purposes and try to preen the hackle back into its original flare when the fly is picked up, whether releasing a fish or otherwise. It is also an excellent practice to check the hook's point and barb at this time. The angler never lived who wasn't done in at one time or another by an unsuspected "hookless hook," that is, one with a broken or turned up point. These mishaps should become rare if you make hook checks a frequent habit. Pretreatment of your fly, particularly the hackles, with dry-fly dressing is essential. Some of my colleagues prefer a thick silicone oil or paste, and others the thinner "dry cleaner" dips or expensive spray-on floatants. Once a fly is really thoroughly soaked, however, none of these will rejuvenate it wery well. Watch a good dry-fly man in action, and you'll see that he takes almost compulsive care of his fly, very probably tying on a fresh one after catching a fish or two, even if the original is still capable of floating. This is one of the advantages in carrying several flies in the same pattern and size.

It isn't hard to figure out that something's wrong when an astronomical strike/hook ratio develops, and while I don't feel that one need slavishly compute ratios all day, it will pay if you'll just keep an eye on the trout's reactions to one fly or another. Watch out for those days when you're getting a so-so ratio of 3 or 4 to 1, and don't be lulled into complacency. Let's assume that a hypothetical fisherman catches six trout in two hours while counting a total of 24 rises to his fly, not bad fishing, really. But what if that 4 to 1 ratio could be converted to, say 1.5 to 1, by means of a simple change such as those described? A little grade school arithmetic shows that he might well triple his catch! So don't live with a mediocre ratio as if it were the status quo; you may be able to improve your luck considerably.

Everyone knows that expert fly fishermen traditionally have lightning-like reflexes, even as do fencing masters and boxers. They need to be quick in order to set their hooks, and so when ratios climb, it's only reasonable to assume that one's reaction time isn't up to par. Indeed, after missing a dozen strikes in a row, anglers may begin to fear that some dread disease is wiping out their reflexes. I've watched a good many people react with some combination of dismay, anger, or bewilderment under circumstances when no amount of added concentration or increased reflex speed would have helped. However, a smaller or drier fly, a thinner tippet, or a different pattern might have! In my opinion, an average set of reflexes is no drawback whatever to becoming an expert dry-fly fisher. When trout are taking deeply and securely, you have all the time in the world to set your hook. There is simply no substitute for a *sincere* strike!

As we have said, trout seldom hook themselves, and many strikes are missed because the angler either isn't trying to watch his fly or can't find it on the water. I think it fair to state that if a fly is worth casting in the first place, it is also worth watching. Many of us fall down in this respect when our fly has already passed through the most intriguing part of its float, although it's not always the angler's fault when he loses sight of his fly. Surface glare will hide the largest artificial, right under your nose, when conditions are bad. Glare is a function of the direction and angle of the sun's rays relative to the water surface, becoming worse when the sun is low and on days with a high, bright overcast. It's often possible to largely escape the glare by casting upstream at an angle, across stream, or even across and down, if necessary, rather than straight up. As mentioned earlier, casting from an elevated bank may also help, for this changes the angle of incident light. Polarizing sun glasses together with a broad hat brim are also invaluable aids in fly watching, but, still and all, you're going to lose a proportion of flies from view. When this happens after what seemed to have been a good cast, don't give up on the fly. It's possible to *guess* at its location fairly accurately if you have watched the line and back part of the leader come down. Just imagine a bushel basket or even a bathtub-sized area about where your fly *should be* and "de-focus" your gaze so as to cover this zone. Surprisingly enough, peripheral vision will usually pick up a rise in the general area in time for an effective strike on your part.

Every fisherman loses flies in one way or another. In my own case, of those I lose, about 30 percent end up in a snag of some sort, usually high in a tree following an unsuccessful strike. It's pretty dumb to throw an ordinary backcast up into a tree, but when a rise comes along, you have to strike back without worrying about what's behind. The other 70 percent end up in a trout's jaw, and almost always as the result of a tippet that breaks on the strike rather than later during the battle. It's the sudden jerk that does the damage. As I see the problem of the snapping tippet, there are five factors involved: (1) the force of the angler's strike, (2) tippet caliber, (3) tippet condition with regard to wear and the presence or absence of wind knots, (4) the size of the trout, and (5) the direction and force of the *trout's strike.* Of these, the first three are under the fisherman's control, although there are often limits to his options insofar as tippet selection is concerned. The wind knot is already familiar, but let me say again that just one of these little devils weakens a tippet by *at least* one X value, and if the knot is in the last few inches close to the fly, the area of greatest wear, it may well test out at only a small fraction of its original rating.

Occasional 15-second breaks taken out of your fishing day add up to time well spent as insurance against: (1) the sodden, poorly floating fly in need of some blotting attention, if not replacement; (2) the broken or blunted hook; and (3) the wounded, weakened tippet.

Assuming that the tippet is in good shape, I believe you'll notice clear-cut differences between 3X and 4X and also between 4X and 5X in the process of everyday fishing. Tippets from 3X on up are plenty tough, and you can safely set your hook with a fairly crisp snap. This doesn't mean catapulting the trout onto the bank, but still a snappy back-sweep of the rod that drives the hook home. However, if you strike this hard on a 4X tippet, you very well may break the trout off, especially if he's good sized or is diving away from you with vigor. And when it comes to 5X and finer tippets, I'd forget about snapping or driving the hook home altogether. In other words, I simply plan to take out all of the slack from my line and leader as briskly as possible, counting on the rod's spring plus the force of the trout's blow to set the hook. The trout's weight and the force of his strike against the rod should be sufficient to drive in a small, sharp hook of the type you'll be using on fine tippets. When changing from a heavier to a finer tippet, I may break off the first trout or two by striking too hard; it's a matter of getting a feel for what a given tippet can stand. Obviously, it's best to err on the side of "gentleness," although this isn't always an easy piece of advice to follow when things get exciting!

Caution notwithstanding, there is a certain amount of luck involved. I almost felt sorry for myself some years ago in the spectacular Lewis River Canyon in Yellowstone, when I lost three out of three nice trout on broken tippets. These fish hit in large pools, and each time I was standing on an elevated rocky bank, and I got a good look at them as they attacked. The first two broke fresh, knot-free, 4X tippets, and the third, a new 3X tippet, by heaving themselves half out of the water and power diving on the helpless fly with tremendous force. The leaders were severed as cleanly as if the fish had carried scissors, and yet my own strike was gentle in each instance, certainly more so than my remarks at the time! For that matter, I've been "done in" by trout I never saw at all. I was wading up the Encampment River in southern Wyoming one day, when I came upon a Volkswagen-sized boulder that looked as if it might shield a good pocket on the far side. I couldn't really see without showing myself, so I lobbed the fly out of sight, over and around the rock by means of a slack, curve cast. There was an instantaneous splash of such proportions that I very nearly dropped the rod! I even glanced at the near bank to see if some practical joker had tossed in a rock (a trick we used to play on one another as youngsters). About that time, the leader reappeared from behind the boulder, needless to say, without my fly. I began to wonder if someone had stocked Piranhas into the usually placid Encampment. (What happened when I threw another fly behind the rock? Not a thing; I never saw the big fly filcher.)

SLACK-LINE CONTROL

Have you ever been on the verge of accomplishing some goal or completing a difficult task only to make a mistake at the last instant and ruin the whole thing? Misadventures that occur at the end of a series of steps pointing toward success are particularly hard to live with. The two-foot putt that hangs on the rim of the cup, turning a par into a bogey, is a familiar example, and beginning fly fishermen soon learn about an equally disastrous mishap that can rob them of a hard-earned trout. An angler goes through a more or less regular series of steps in the process of pursuing a fish, that is, reading the water, figuring the float, approaching and casting, etc. If his moves up to this point have been appropriate, he will hopefully see a rise, set the hook, and land his quarry. It's a very natural reflex to strike back when a trout accosts your fly, and while trout sometimes take the fly deep, hitting it hard enough and at an angle such that they hook themselves, it's ordinarily necessary to bring the rod's spring into play before the hook will penetrate. The crux of the matter is that during the process of casting, slack accumulates in the line, and there is a limit to the amount of slack that can be taken up in attempting to set the hook. If there is too much slack, the line can't be pulled taut, the hook won't go home, and the angler has lost his fish; that's all there is to it!

Slack can form in several areas. It predictably builds up in the back part of the line just beyond the rod. Some of this slack may be left over from the forward cast, but most of it develops as the fly floats back to the angler from above; the longer the float, the more the slack builds. Some, perhaps all, of this slack can be taken up by briskly sweeping the rod back toward two o'clock on the strike. Reasonable rod length is clearly helpful in this regard, and the angler can also effectively lengthen the rod by extending his arm so that the rod comes back high. The left hand can further

assist by pulling in line at the same time, just as in lifting off for a backcast, but still there's only so much slack that you can eliminate on a strike.

Secondly, slack is essentially stored between the lowest line guide and the reel. Rather than keeping the line more or less tight between the reel and rod, most fishermen allow a group of loose coils to form at their feet while they work the line in and out during a series of casts. When they make a longer throw, line is borrowed from this supply, and if the cast is a shorter one, more line is stored. There is nothing wrong with this system, everyone uses it. However, there has to be some sort of clamp on the line close to the last guide, if the angler is to set his hook. Otherwise, when he whips the rod back, it will pick up only the loosest slack, that is, the slack line that is least well anchored. In this setting, an extended forward cast lying out on the water is almost always better fixed than the loose coils in front of the reel, and so the rod moves the wrong end of the line without budging the fly at all. Of course, there's no problem so long as your left hand has a grip on the line when you strike, but in the beginning, it's easy to forget that you have a left hand. For instance, many fishermen shoot some line on a majority of their casts. I described the left hand's role in this regard only up to the point of releasing its hold for the shoot, leaving it suspended in mid-air, so to speak. The left hand needs to regain its grip as soon as possible, and yet this is a time of intense preoccupation for the angler. He has made his pitch, the fly has fluttered into the water, fly and target are growing ever closer, and it's no trick to conjure up visions of lurking lunkers. Unfortunately, this is no time for daydreams, and while it is essential to watch the terminal tackle, one must also keep tabs on the uninteresting back part of the line.

I recall a frustrating afternoon spent with my 11-year old son on the Big Wood

River below Sun Valley, Idaho. I hoped the boy might have enough success on this bright summer day to divert his attention from frogs to fish, and was delighted to come upon a trout-filled feeding riffle some 60 yards in length. Starting him at the downstream end, I forded and climbed atop a boulder to watch. The choppy surface allowed the youngster to get away with short 15 to 20 foot casts, and sure enough, his floating Royal Wulff was getting clobbered on nearly every presentation. Young Bill saw most of the rises, reacting with commendable quickness, but no amount of wrenching and heaving on the rod could get the line taut. In fact, 70 exciting although fishless minutes passed before a small Rainbow managed to hook himself. The boy was casting a fair amount of slack because of a slight breeze; however, the big problem was his inability to remember his left hand. Bill seemed to be hypnotized by the sight of the dancing fly as it bounced along over the riffle, knowing that a trout would strike at any instant; he continually dropped the line, leaving his left hand dangling uselessly. I've no idea how many trout a more mature angler might have taken from that riffle, possibly twenty, but interestingly, the youngster did much better as the afternoon wore on and action slowed. After he could no longer count on a strike with each cast, he seemed better able to concentrate on line control. I can understand this, because I too sometimes forget the rear slack in the process of completing an especially difficult cast or when my fly is floating through particularly provocative water. I find myself admiring the float of the fly, my left hand flapping in the breeze very much like a youngster's, and I pay the same price!

Rear slack can cause double trouble by creating an entirely different kind of problem involving an insidious type of drag. Suppose that an angler comes upon a little waterfall formed by rocks strewn across the stream at right angles to the channel. Brush has piled against the upstream side of the falls, forming a placid pool above. A good fish is rising some 30 feet upstream in the pool, and in order to keep his profile low, our angler makes his cast from the base of the falls. The fly flutters down gently on the end of a shallow curve, some 10 seconds float time above the trout and right on target. The trout starts for the fly as the fisherman holds his breath, but suddenly his fly lurches into a sickening downstream drag. Now how could this happen if the entire cast covered water with uniformly slow current? Of course, all of the line was originally cast over slow water, but as the fly floated down, so did the rear part of the line until it was caught by the accelerating current at the lip of the falls and sucked over. Our fisherman has lost all chance of taking this fish, the entire pool is likely ruined, his fly has drowned, and to top it off, his line, leader, and fly will soon be tangled in a maze of brush inside the waterfall! He'll likely be wet up to the shoulder on one side by the time this mess is unraveled.

Little waterfalls aren't common on most streams; however, on a reduced scale, this sort of problem arises quite frequently. Rear slack may cause drag whenever the angler is standing in or just in front of water with a current different from that in the target area. This also includes situations where the rear line gets anchored in slack water that impedes the fly's float along a swifter current. These problems can be avoided by tucking away slack as it accumulates beyond the rod tip with your left hand and also by simply lifting the rear line off the surface with the rod! Rear line can't very well cause drag when it's up in the air (except possibly when caught by a strong wind). A longer rod is most helpful for lifting quantities of line free, just as in taking up slack on a strike, and an extended arm again affords extra leverage for this purpose. Small swift streams tend to present a great deal of fine detail; three or four currents running in somewhat different directions and at different speeds may be jammed into a narrow strip of water between pockets of slack. This is precisely the kind of spot in which rod lift is so important. In fact, when working in very tight quarters with casts of 15 feet or less, I often lift the whole line plus the back half of the leader free! You can do this without disturbing the fly's float if the tippet is sufficiently flexible. In addition, I sometimes use a primitive "dapping" method that hardly qualifies as a fly cast for getting my fly into a close target. If you raise the rod high enough so that the line and leader swing back and forth, front to back below the rod like a pendulum, the rod can flip the fly and a few inches of tippet into the target at the end of an outward swing. The idea of lifting rear slack free may seem too obvious for comment, but I've seen countless fishermen valiantly attempting to beat the drag with fancy casts, when all they really needed was to get that rear slack off the water! I've noticed that most of the fatigue I pick up in my arm and shoulder after a long day on the stream comes from rod lifting rather than actual casting. Surely there isn't anything very difficult about slack line control; it's much more of a habit than a skill, and veterans do it automatically. Perhaps this is why the topic so seldom appears in books and articles on fly fishing.

Rear slack is easily removed by a busy left hand and stored. So long as there is a "stop" on the stored slack, there's no danger, although if the rear slack accumulates rapidly, as in a swift current, you may wish to use the index and third fingers of your rod hand as an extra, bottom line guide. Here the line is loosely trapped between your fingers and the rod grip while the left hand strips in slack. In this way, when the left arm has pulled in a full sweep of line, your left hand can release its hold and take another grip close to the lowest line guide (in this case, the "living" finger guide) without fear that there will be a strike *during* the transfer. If a strike should come along while the left hand is in transit, the fingers simply clamp down. I must admit that I sometimes gamble by not protecting my left hand in this way, although there are days when the trout appear to be able to time their strikes so that they hit just at the instant I reach for a fresh hand hold. It costs me a fish almost every time, too!

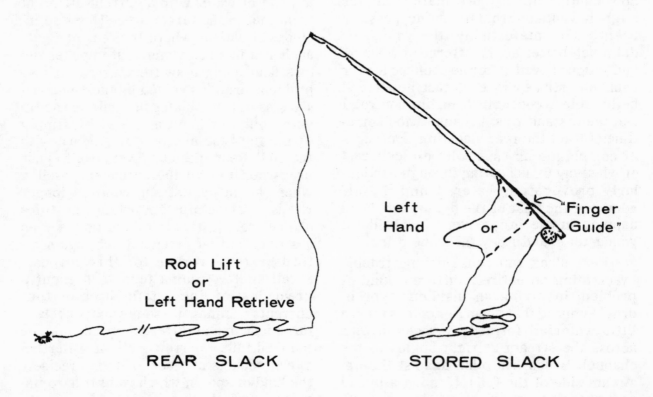

Rod Lift
or
Left Hand Retrieve

REAR SLACK

Left Hand   or   "Finger Guide"

STORED SLACK

The Indispensable Wet Flies

I once met a man who had some pretty strong ideas about the best way to learn to become a good fly fisherman. He had his three sons in tow along the North Platte in Wyoming, and imposed a strict rule to the effect that each boy must begin the day by catching a certain number of trout on wet flies. As I recall, the quota was three fish. After that goal had been achieved, the pupil could then switch to dry flies if he wished. In other words, they had to *earn* dry-fly privileges. It was very much like making the youngsters finish their vegetables before taking on the dessert course, and at the time, the fellow seemed something of a tyrant. I've since realized that he wanted the boys to become will balanced, "complete" anglers, recognizing that the palatable dry fly is potentially habit forming. After all, the floaters do offer a great deal of excitement and are technically easy to manage, and so it's no wonder that people become addicted to them. I suspect that this rigid father would have agreed with my own view to the effect that most dry-fly purists get to be that way simply because they've never learned to fish a wet fly effectively! A highly compelling observation backs up the man's "wet before dry" rule: there is just no escaping the fact that on some occasions wet flies give the floaters a sound whipping in head-on competition between equally competent anglers, and these are not rare events! The dry-fly purist is like a workman attempting to do a job with a partial set of tools; sooner or later, he must surely pay the price, unless he is willing and able to highly restrict his fishing. For instance, I recall a particularly fastidious angler who belonged to an exclusive club on the South Platte River, less than a two hours drive from Denver. This fortunate fellow could determine what the trout were up to by simply phoning the keeper before venturing forth, and he did virtually all of his fishing for the season on that single stretch of water. He fished a lot, but only during the best dry-fly months, heading for home if conditions became unfavorable. For my own part, I greatly enjoy watching seasonal changes unfold, learning to cope with them, and visiting the widest variety of waters possible. An angler with these preferences just has to become a "two-way" fisherman if he is to prosper; purism is not a practical alternative. In reviewing my log book for the past three seasons, I find that out of a total of 100 fishing days, I used wet flies exclusively on 27, dry flies exclusively on 33, and both during the remaining 40 days, a fairly even balance, spanning from April into November.

Quite apart from taking more fish at certain times, many two-way fly fishers also believe that wets take larger trout in the long run. In my experience, they have more than held their own in this regard. Many anglers go through a sort of maturation process wherein they become more interested in capturing a relatively modest number of good trout than in catching a mess of ordinary fish. I know that this motive clearly influences my choice of flies on many an occasion. Finally, there is the intangible but very real satisfaction for the competent wet-fly fisherman of knowing that he has a skill possessed by a relative few of his competitors.

Wet-fly terminology is somewhat confusing. The traditional wet fly was designed to mimic a drowned adult fly, and the artificial nymph copies an immature larval or pupal form of an aquatic insect. Nonetheless, some patterns such as the popular Grey Hackle Yellow, Mosquito, and Black Gnat make fine nymph imitations; at least, I suspect that the trout usually take them as such. Therefore, the distinction between wet fly and nymph is often a superficial one. Take the deservedly famous Wooly Worm series of wet flies. Originally tied to simulate caterpillars, wooly worms are more often fished as nymphs in waters devoid of caterpillars, and with deadly effect.

A sodden dry fly can be presented half

submerged in the surface film as an imitation of a drowning adult or hatching nymph, and thus it functionally becomes a wet fly. There are even double-duty patterns such as the well-known Muddler Minnow. The bulky Muddler is actually a streamer wet fly, but it's also a favorite floating grasshopper imitation when treated with dry-fly dressing, and so strict definitions pertaining to fly types are neither necessary nor terribly useful.

There are certain identifiable situations in which sunken flies are likely to prove especially effective. High water brings accelerated flow with racing currents that scour the stream bed and banks, tearing loose various types of food that wouldn't ordinarily be awash. Following a summer storm, earthworms and other bank dwellers become available to the trout, as do nymphs that have lost their hold on the bottom. This is hardly news to the bait clan, nor should it be to those of us who prefer the fly. On occasion, I have even been guilty of the unorthodox (if not uncouth) practice of fishing a nymph that happens to suggest a plain old worm! Specifically, the Atherton nymph (medium shade) has a body of beige fur dubbing with just a touch of pink, and when tied on a large, long shanked hook, this fly has the diameter, length, and color of a stubby earth-worm. One August day, a torrential rain chased us from flooded rivers into the high grassy meadows near historic Cumbres Pass in southern Colorado, but even here, the meandering streams were running over their banks. It looked as if we fly fishers were out of luck until, for no particular reason, I tied on an Atherton. Two hours later it had taken 18 trout! The few we killed were stuffed with worms, and I'm sure that a regular "garden hackle" would have been good too, although hardly better, for a single bedraggled nymph did all of the damage for me. Real worms don't wear nearly so well! Interestingly, darker wet flies were poor in this brimming brook, while dry flies flunked altogether.

Very cold water also points up the value of wet flies. Since trout are cold blooded, their "thermostats" get turned way down by frigid water and they become inactive. Hatches are unlikely, too, because insect life is similarly affected; hence the torpid trout are content to lie in their holding water and are reluctant to bestir themselves for surface rises. Nymphs, however, may be able to save what was expected to be a dry-fly day when temperatures dive. The Conejos is one of Colorado's prettiest rivers, much favored by dry-fly fishermen, particularly after the multitudes of summer visitors are gone, and groves of golden aspen decorate its steep canyon walls. Your timing has to be just right for these fall trips, because the first wintery storm can scramble the fishing situation completely, even after it has passed. Snowmelt from the massive peaks which surround the headwaters sends stream temperatures skidding into the upper 30s and lower 40s, stunning the river into at least temporary hibernation. Nonetheless, I've been able to salvage reasonable fishing on these occasions by probing the deep holding water with wet flies. In this way, the trout can take my artificial with an absolute minimum of effort, if they have any interest at all in feeding. This sort of home delivery service beats any amount of futile flailing with dry flies; I've tried both!

Wets are particularly valuable in the early season when high swift waters and low temperatures both prevail. There is an excellent biological explanation since a stream behaves very much like a watery garden at this time of year. Its animal and vegetable inhabitants essentially begin to "come up" or "bloom" as the days grow longer and warmer. Indeed, these forms of life do form anew in the manner of annual crops, and so it happens that the nymphs of many species become active prior to their emergence, seeming to abound in increasing numbers. Under these circumstances, one can try to match the "pre-hatch," so to speak, with appropriate nymphs. It may be possible to identify such nymphs swimming or drifting in the current, or perhaps scrambling along the bottom. This may require a little sleuthing, however, for a certain nymph can be prevalent without becoming particularly obvious. One May morning, I spent three fruitless hours nymphing the rugged canyon of the Tarryall River just above its junction with the South Platte, not far from Denver. When a large number of nymph patterns failed to bring so much as a strike, it occurred to me that perhaps I should try to use my head more, and the rod less. Setting my tackle aside, I began to dredge the bottom in search of naturals by scooping up handfulls of sandy gravel and turning over rocks. At first my efforts disclosed just a few Caddis cases and small May fly larvae. Then, a half-sunken willow branch out in the swiftest current caught my eye, and wrenching it free, I tossed the tangle of twigs and moss onto the bank for closer inspection. Amazingly, it was literally swarming with dark, reddish-brown Stone fly nymphs up to an inch and a quarter in length. I hadn't seen an adult all day! Returning the Stone fly nursery to the river, I vainly searched my fly boxes for an imitation. Everything I had was either too small or too light colored, and I headed for home with an empty creel after sacrificing several of the big fellows in a small bottle of vodka (carried for such emergencies). I returned several days later after a session at my tying vise, armed with matching nymphs. The big artificials were gratifyingly successful this time, and to complete the picture, I found numerous naturals in the trout's stomachs together with scattered adults resting in the willows. In this instance, the clue to an effective fly in terms of size, color, and configuration (long and slender bodied) came from study of the stream for naturals.

The content of a trout's stomach sometimes provides this kind of information more quickly and easily. There can hardly be better proof of what they are taking! The following spring, I tackled the main South Platte, again depending on my Stone fly imitation. This time, however, it let me down completely in the cold, swift waters, and eventually I gave up on the fly. I fished with other patterns for quite some time, until at long last, a nice Brown tagged a black nymph tied with a white underside. I rather expected to find an empty stomach in view of my notable lack of success, but surprisingly, the Brown's belly and gullet were crammed with stubby, grub-like larvae about an inch in length. These pale, dirty grey creatures had tiny legs clustered at one end below a small head and I realized that they were the "rock worms" or nymphs of the Crane fly that I had read about in Schwiebert's book. The larvae are actually harvested along the Platte by enterprising locals for sale to early season bait fishers. The clumsy, heavy bodies of the rock worms, combined with feeble legs, equip them poorly for withstanding the heavy waters of the runoff, and they are easily washed out of slack water into currents. Working together, two collectors sometimes pair off in a manner such that the upstream member kicks up rocks and debris from the bottom while the other holds a screen below to catch dislodged rock worms. Spidery, long-legged adult Crane flies have relatively little fishing value since they dart about in clusters high above the water, but on certain streams such as the Platte, the immature forms are another matter.

NATURAL STONEFLY NYMPH

TURKEY FEATHER WING CASE
BROWN QUILL BODY

DUBBED SEAL HAIR GILLS &
BROWN PARTRIDGE HACKLE

Fortunately, this time I happened to have a couple of reasonable nymph copies in the miscellaneous section of my fly book, and they soon changed a slow day into a fast one. Nor was there any doubt that the trout were actively feeding on Crane fly larvae, for of the five fish I killed, each was chock-full. Apparently, the white underside of the black nymph led that first Brown to strike, and thereafter an artificial tied with a fat body of grey-white fur dubbing and fished dead drift did the trick nicely. I profited from this discovery for several weeks thereafter, and unlike the bait fishers, I had no need for window screens, boxes of wet moss, or frequent timeouts to replace the fragile naturals on my hook!

In each of the preceding examples, a little knowledge of trout-related insect life was helpful, and could have been more so. For instance, I should have remembered that Stone fly nymphs are generally early season hatchers and live exclusively in fast water, for I nearly neglected to search the currents. Then, preoccupied with these Stone fly nymphs, I forgot what I knew about Crane fly larvae the following spring. The point is that one can gradually accumulate an invaluable store of data of this type. Once an angler has a fix on one or another natural in a certain stream at a specific time of the season, he can zero in with patterns that stand a good chance of success. Of course, the same applies to floating food as well, although adult insects are generally a good deal more obvious than their nymphs.

I suggested earlier that dry-fly fishing can become good following a storm when water conditions begin to improve, but wet flies are probably an even better bet at such times. Goaded by a temporary bonanza of food, newly liberated by the high water, and shielded by the roil, trout may really turn on just as soon as the water is clear enough to give them a little visibility.

We have talked about high water, cold water, dirty water, and early season thus far, as if one should fish wets only when conditions are "non-dry fly." As a matter of fact, many anglers do live by this simple philosophy, always giving floaters the first shot. Nor can you fault them. After all, theirs is a practical approach, since adequate execution of dry-fly technique often requires less effort and concentration. But assuming that the trout will take either on *or* beneath the surface (as is so often the case), does the dry fly always win out? By no means; wets may well come off with the honors, even in the midst of a hatch as in an episode on the Big Laramie River near the Wyoming-Colorado border. We had been the happy beneficiaries of two days of marvelous dry-fly fishing when on the morning of the third day, our luck mysteriously ran out. The weather remained fine, and I had a feeling that things were about to break loose as the day wore on, but it was well into the afternoon before the first surface rises appeared. Then my premonition suddenly came true, for within five minutes, trout were coming up all over the river and in water of every type. I puzzled as to what set them off. Then, as I released the fourth of a series of rather small Browns, a plump grey May fly dun floated by my hand, valiantly struggling to become airborne. And so I had my answer, but where were they hatching? I could see a half-dozen different kinds of water as to depth, current, and bottom in my vicinity. Surely these big duns weren't hatching everywhere at once? While kneeling in the shallows to release my next customer, I happened to glance downriver in such a way that the water was silhouetted against a bright blue summer sky. I did a double take, for there appeared to be a definite cluster of flies over the central channel current within a few feet of the surface. Hurrying down the bank, I fought my way out to the tail of the channel in hopes of getting at some better fish. At first I wondered if I had seen a mirage of some sort. The duns were almost invisible at close range against the glare, and when I fired a Grey Wulff into the teeth of the current, a tough surface rip promptly drowned the ordinarily buoyant fly. Nonetheless, I saw a good fish flash at the Wulff as it raced by, half sunken, and wondered what their response might be to a nymph fished in or just below the surface film. I could get away with a very short line, thanks to the choppy water, and so bracing my feet between two rocks, I teetered in the current while switching to a shorter, heavier leader and a no. 12 blue dun nymph. This fly was tied with a body of dyed seal's fur and speckled, grey Guinea Fowl hackle. The size and color should match the nymph pretty well, I thought, judging from the dun, and the shaggy body was "buggy" from an impressionistic viewpoint. I was not disappointed, for while the hatch lasted, I had a Brown of at least 12 inches on my line or was wading back into position after chasing one of the lusty fighters downstream. This is not a dramatic tale, but an everyday sort of experience wherein I essentially traded a smaller number of good fish (to 15 inches) for what would probably have been a larger catch of pan sizers, a swap that most of us would make any time!

In discussing dry-fly fishing, I purposely avoided a rather important issue. There are times when selective, surface-feeding trout refuse any and all imitations, and yet rise heavily to naturals that one cannot see. In these maddening situations, we usually assume that the naturals are just too small to be visible, but there is another very good possibility. The target insects may actually be slightly below or even clinging to the underside of the surface film rather than on top of it, and in this case, a shallowly fished or only semi-sunken wet fly can turn an apparently hopeless situation completely around. Hatching May fly nymphs are not the only culprits; indeed, there are innumerable candidates, including the larvae of two-winged flies such as the gnats, aquatic beetles, freshwater shrimp, and Caddis pupae.

Now and then, observations of insect life along the banks can be translated into very good wet-fly fishing, since land dwellers are no less interesting to the trout than are aquatic nymphs when they become available. I have recorded several anecdotal examples of this sort, featuring the ever-present ant and succulent caterpillar in upcoming chapters.

To summarize, it seems to me that one ought to be prepared (both physically and mentally) to fish a wet fly under all sorts of conditions, whether dictated by water temperature, the calendar, or observations of insect life along, within, or even above the water. The wets are truly "flies for all seasons!"

Insofar as pattern selection is concerned, there are probably more wet flies than dries, and to make matters more complicated, wet-fly patterns are less standardized. I went through a period of infatuation with the idea that meticulously matching nymph patterns were a necessity, but as in the case of dry flies, I've turned to impressionistic patterns for the most part. Certainly, one can't go far wrong by developing confidence in a small number of patterns that are acceptable to the trout under a wide range of conditions. It makes sense to pay careful attention to recommendations concerning regional or seasonal favorites in an unfamiliar locale. In fact, one of the hottest tips of this kind I've received involved a stream I thought I

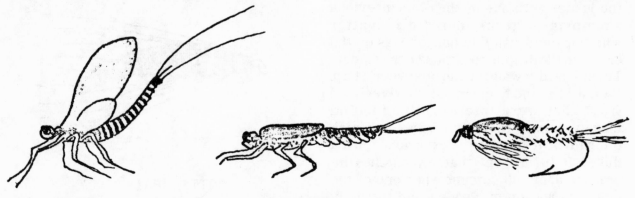

DUN... suggested → NYMPH... suggested → FLY

knew thoroughly. Our annual trek into the White River Wilderness took place late in July at a time when the river was still somewhat high, and while a number of skilled dry-fly men plied their wares, wet flies still produced the most and largest fish. Over a period of almost 20 years, two patterns, the Grey Hackle Yellow and the Royal Coachman, had emerged as consistent favorites. Then, while at school, I met a fellow who had been reared on a ranch along the William's Fork of the Yampa River, a stream much like our own, that also headed on the high White River Plateau. An avid angler, he was a staunch advocate of the Pott's Hair Flies. I had never heard of these patterns, but since the two rivers were so similar, I stopped by a tackle shop one day to check them out. When the clerk finally found the box of Pott's Flies on a dusty back shelf, I could see why sales had been slow. Tied with woven horse hair, the ungainly creations more resembled small whisk brooms than trout flies! The proprietor was discontinuing the line and was anxious to sell me all I wanted at cost; however, I settled for a single fly in the Lady Mite and Sandy Mite patterns. As it happened, I forgot about the "horse flies," as I called them, until most of the next year's trip was over. When the Lady Mite eventually got a chance to show its stuff, it put on a remarkable performance. In those days, I fished two flies on the same leader, the upper attached by means of a dropper loop three feet above the leader tip. Of 47 consecutive trout landed, the Lady Mite took 41 while sharing the leader with one of the other previous champion patterns, nor did it matter whether the brush-like hair fly was on the end or in the dropper position on the leader! I could hardly wait for the next year's trip. Would I be able to clean out the river? Did trout that were interested in feeding merely survey the pair of flies and pick their favorite, or was the experience just a fluke? It turned out that my catches increased about 40 percent when one of the hair flies was on my leader, and the daily ratio favoring the Pott's fly varied from 2 to 1 up to as much as 6 to 1! Was there an

explanation? Thinking back, Caddis flies were always plentiful on the South Fork, darting over the water and fluttering within the brush, although the trout paid scant attention to them insofar as surface rises were concerned. I was largely ignorant of stream-side entomology in those days, but I suspect that these Caddis crawled out along the banks to hatch rather than emerging in open water, and thus weren't available to the trout. However, the free-swimming Caddis pupa, the immature form between the larva and the adult fly, has long trailing legs and antennae, very much like the stiff, bristly conformation of the Pott's flies. The color and size match happened to be quite close too, and further, the trout sometimes hit an actively manipulated nymph with great eagerness, as if it were a swimming pupa. I suspect that there are always sound biological reasons behind trout's feeding preferences among fly patterns, if we can only identify them!

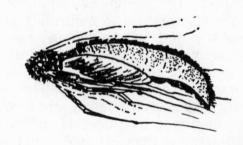

CADDIS PUPA

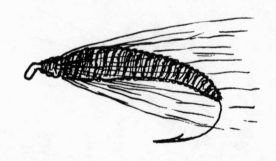

POTTS HAIR FLY

Of course, wet-fly size is critical as in the example quoted earlier when all of my flies were too small to effectively copy swarming Stone fly nymphs of the Tarryall River. The opposite sort of mismatch can defeat you too. The concept of enticing the trout with a big mouthful, that is a large fly, is psychologically appealing, but beware—this kind of thinking can do you out of some otherwise splendid fishing! It was my firm intention one summer afternoon to relieve Idaho's Big Lost River of one or several of its heavy Rainbows with the aid of a minnow-sized fly. I planned to work deep, utilizing the primitive (and probably prehistoric) philosophy that big fish want big lures. My confidence grew when we met two spin fishermen returning from the river with several beauties they had taken on spoons. Unfortunately, I paid attention only to the positive part of their story at the time. I should also have remembered another aspect, for they indicated that the river had been dead since noon. I'd hardly gotten underway when a lengthy Rainbow rolled past my deep-sweeping streamer, apparently missing his strike. As you might imagine, that fly visited the depths of all manner of provocative channels and pools during the next hour, but that fish was the only one I saw; big nymphs did not do any better. A bit tired and thoroughly discouraged, I rested on the bank, waiting for something to happen and idly watching the air space above the water. I'd noticed tiny darting objects over the stream on several occasions, moving in a curiously vertical fashion toward the surface. Aside from a few pale Caddis flies fluttering about, there was little to see. Then, suddenly, one of the little Caddis dived headlong into the water! Now the pieces of this piscatorial puzzle began to fit together. The females of certain Caddis species lay their eggs by power diving through the surface film, depositing the eggs on a submerged object before swimming back to the surface or clambering out onto a rock. Evidently, this was precisely what had been going on, for you could see most of the Caddis dive if you watched them long enough. Taking the hint, we tried wet flies. Every small, pale-colored wet fly we fished was devastating, either presented dead drift or via a drag retrieve. I strongly suspect that the antics of these Caddis had spoiled the spin fishers' sport and that the big Rainbow I'd seen was after a swimming Caddis rather than my streamer. I was probably fortunate not to have seen more fish flash by my hefty, trophy-hunting flies, else I might have stuck with them longer. When large naturals such as the Stone and Crane fly nymphs are around, there may be real feeding explosions, and it's only common sense to go with big flies, but remember that many (and in fact most) of nature's creations are more dainty. Expert wet-fly fishers are not at all reluctant to work with no. 18s and even smaller imitations in dealing with some of the midget May flies, Caddis flies, gnats, and beetles. It's well to emphasize that insects which create a "pseudo dry-fly" rise clinging to the surface film are usually pretty small.

I'm not interested in pushing my own pattern preferences, although I will mention several favorites of impressionistic type. The *Zug Bug* is a simple fly that employs glistening, dark green peacock herl for the body, together with mottled brown feather tails, wing cases, and hackle. A skillful angler friend, who really prefers wet to dry flies, put me on to the *Martinez Black* and beige *medium Atherton* patterns. Both utilize glossy fur-dubbed bodies with a thin tinsel ribbing and bright wing cases. Like the sheen of the peacock herl, these materials make for effective impressionism. A beginner could do worse than to stock up on the ever-popular and easily available Wooly Worms in black, brown, orange, and yellow. Little more than hooks wrapped with pipe cleaners and overwrapped with soft hackle feathers, these are universally popular flies. There are countless others, of which some feature bodies of woven fabric and some are intricately molded in plastic. My own preference is for shaggy-bodied, ragged-looking flies, usually incorporating fur, and lacking sharply detailed markings such as two-toned bodies, precisely jointed legs, and the like.

SLACK-LINE STRIKING:
A PSYCHOLOGICAL HURDLE

There is no doubt that among fly fishers this skill separates the men from the boys more than any other. I can vividly recall the helpless feeling I got when my fly disappeared into the depths of some green pool, drifting slack and completely "out of contact." It's just plain hard to live with the frustrating realization that unknowingly, the best trout of your career may be mouthing the hidden fly at that very instant, before spitting it out in disgust. In the early days, I became discouraged by this apparently hopeless situation all too quickly, and turned from natural drifts to the security of a drag retrieve. Understandably, this is not the way to learn to set the hook on a slack line, and further, dependency on drag retrieves is a bad habit, if not an outright weakness. It boils down to deciding that you want to, can, and *will* master slack-line striking; it is a decision that's going to require a certain amount of faith plus a good deal of patience, practice, and concentration. You will have to put out some effort, but I have absolutely no reservations in stating that the skill gain is well worth the price. Not only will you catch a good many fish that would have refused a dragged wet fly, but there is also the feeling of accomplishment that comes with learning a less than simple technique. This is why I am so highly respectful of those bait fishers who work dead drift. They can slack-line strike with the very best, a fact that should dampen any tendency toward snobbery that we fly fishers may develop!

Looking back, I suppose that I sort of eased into slack lining by seeking out current targets I could fish "sidesaddle." Positioning myself across stream from the target and casting quartering and upstream, I was careful to select spots that were free of glare from this angle, and I tried to keep my casts as short as possible. Cross-current presentations have a strong potential for drag, but if you can lick this problem, they have the advantage of building a minimum of slack during the float. Thus, at close range, I had excellent visibility coupled with a fairly straight leader, and in clear water, it was possible to trace the leader almost all the way to my fly. I then focused intently on the leader, as far out as I could see it, and waited for a shadow to dart toward the area where I know my fly should be, a foot or two beyond. I learned that if I struck the instant the leader did "something funny" (that is, changed its float pattern in some manner), I was very likely to be into a fish. In this way, I gradually convinced myself that trout really do hit free-floating flies and can be hooked, if I simply watched the leader. Handling a dead drift off a straight upstream cast with rapidly accumulating slack took more practice, but you have to start somewhere.

Slack-line striking is easy enough to describe, but can be learned only on the water. Therefore, the following remarks amount to a bit of encouragement sprinkled with a few suggestions, for words alone won't do the trick. Basically, an angler only has to watch the terminal tackle for any change in the *direction* of drift or *speed* of drift, either singly or in combination. I emphasized direction and speed, although the key word here is really *change*, because these changes, whatever their nature, often signal a trout's take. Just as in their reactions to floaters, trout also attack wet flies with varying degrees of vim and vigor. There are those happy days when they literally slug the fly, as well as the more trying occasions when they seem to merely nuzzle it. Consequently, the visual signals that indicate a strike come in a variety of intensities. For instance, assume that the leader suddenly stops floating toward you and actually reverses course, darting backward. This is the obvious signal of a hard strike, and one that should be perfectly apparent to anyone, so long as he is watching for it. But suppose that the same leader simply comes to a stop in its float? This signal is not so plain, and although an experienced person should pick it up instantly, a beginner might puzzle long enough to miss his fish. Finally, the leader might only slow a little in its drift, bringing the angler a much less conspicuous message. Similarly, leaders may veer suddenly and sharply to either side of their drift route, or dip downward—but how suddenly and how sharply, how much veer or dip? Here again there is a spectrum of signal intensities from the very clear ones to a really subtle set of messages.

It's easy to see why intense concentration and the best possible visibility are prerequisites to success. It is also important to focus on the visible portion of the tackle chain that's closest to your fly, whether that part be the tippet, mid-leader, leader butt, or the end of the line. The farther out toward the fly one can get a visual fix, the better, because the strike message is essentially telegraphed back along the tackle chain and fades progressively as it travels toward the rod. If the leader has knotted segments (hopefully other than those of the wind variety), the splice knots themselves are handy objects for visual fix. The real zealots go so far as to dab a spot of bright paint on their leaders or wrap a tiny bit of colored plastic tape around them for this purpose. Of course, short casts go a long way toward simplifying leader watching, thanks to proximity—still another payoff for the aggressive approacher! When leader visibility is poor because of murky water or glare, the shortest leader consistent with adequate camouflage is helpful too, for you will likely be watching the line-leader knot rather than the leader per se.

I went on at some length about the strike/hook ratio and ways of improving it in dry-fly fishing. The same considerations apply to wet flies, for it is naturally easier to set the hook when there are slashing strikes of the kind that literally make a leader jump. As before, it's well worth experimenting with different patterns and

hook sizes in an effort to encourage this kind of heavy hitting, although results are generally less obvious than with floaters. It's more difficult to compute a ratio in the case of wet flies, since a number of real strikes are going to be missed by the most expert and observant angler, while other leader hesitations that suggest a strike are in reality the result of a temporary snag on a rock or piece of drift wood. I've found, however, that on any particular occasion the trout tend to follow a trend insofar as the way they are hitting, whether their strikes are bold, shy, or somewhere in between. Unless the trout are really swinging from the heels, I manipulate patterns and sizes long enough to be sure that I can't do better. Sometimes small changes have surprising impact on trout response. There's a pretty brook in the Jemez Mountains west of Santa Fe that I like to fish each spring at a time when there is a fair population of Stone fly nymphs awash in the high waters. One species is dominant, and the mature nymphs that are ready to hatch are large fellows, approximating an artificial tied on a no. 10 long shanked hook. It's only logical to show the trout the most appetizing fly possible, and so I've frequently started out with a slightly bigger than life imitation in a no. 8. Interestingly however, a no. 10 or even a no. 12 nymph has invariably been more effective. For example, last year, I counted 14 strikes that I felt reasonably sure of on a no. 8, hooking three fish in 90 minutes. Changing to a no. 10, I was then able to hook nine trout on 19 strikes in the next hour and a half, thanks to harder, more solid hits. This little experiment impresses me, because if you hold the artificial nymphs in sizes 8 and 10 side by each in your palm, they are very similar indeed, and if examined separately, it's difficult to be sure which is which. Apparently the trout can tell though, and it matters to them!

In the event that visibility is really excellent, why not watch the fly and forget about the leader? Here there are some pros and cons to consider. I made a fool of myself not long ago by fly watching while nymphing the clear, shallow Chama River in northern New Mexico. Its Browns were beautifully camouflaged, but lighting conditions were ideal, and I could see both the fish and my fly so well (I thought) that it was possible to come up with a fairly accurate strike/hook ratio. Mine was a horrible 13 to 1, more or less, and stayed that way despite all manner of fly changes. I developed a severe eye-strain headache after several hours of hard work before I finally figured out what was going on. It took me that long to realize that the buff-colored, cobblestone bottom made the Brownies virtually invisible as they stealthily glided up to my nymph. It wasn't the strike I was seeing at all, but rather their frantic retreat after discovering they had a mouthful of phoney fur and feathers! Hence the horse was already out of the barn by the time I tried to set the hook. I did infinitely better thereafter by simply diverting my attention from the easily followed fly to the splice knot above the tippet. When your cast first hits the water, the leader is much easier to find than the fly in the event of a quick strike, and so I usually try to pick up the leader right away, using it to guide my eye out to the nymph. This way, if an early strike does come along, I'm ready for it. Finally, anglers who allow fly watching to become a habit never learn to recognize tell-tale but subtle leader messages. On the plus side, while focusing on the fly, I have often spotted good trout following my imitation or even striking and missing it, a situation in which a repeat presentation has a good chance of success. Fly and leader watching needn't be mutually exclusive and shouldn't be; try both before deciding which is best in a given setting.

In contrast to the furtive approach of the Browns just described, striking trout often create all sorts of flashes, glints, darting shadows, and indescribable flurries in the water when they take, sort of a set of "visual commotions" in the fly's area. Peripheral vision is truly a remarkable property, and one that can be trained to pick up these signals, even when your gaze is intently concentrated on some portion of the leader. Ray Bergman describes strik-

ing at the shadow of a bird passing overhead, so keenly honed were his reactions to this kind of message. In my own experience, the less obvious strikes have been the most prevalent, and the beginner must be willing to hang in through some slow hours if he is to learn to recognize and react to them. Each successful strike becomes a confidence-building event that gets programmed into a subconscious memory bank (very much in the manner of water reading), a data bank that will eventually function for him in an amazing way. Now and then I'll try to categorize and record the strike signal each time I hook a trout on a natural drift. In other words, I keep tally of just what I saw that led me to strike. Was the signal obvious, of intermediate intensity or more of a vague hunch? Oddly enough, on many days, a majority of successful strikes defy classification, because I have no idea why I reacted, even immediately after the fact! Hence the message that pulled my strike trigger, so to speak, came across at a subconscious level. Perhaps this sounds mystic, a bit like hearing voices from outer space, but countless fishermen have had the same experience. If you have an urge to strike, for whatever reason (or lack of reason), give it a go! There is little to lose even if your catch is nothing more than a water-logged aspen twig. For that matter, I'd give yourself a lot of credit for this sort of "catch." A creel full of drift wood won't impress anyone, but if you can pick up the slight interference with drift caused by the hook scraping across the branch, you're well on your way. Eventually, these snags will more and more frequently come to represent the business end of a trout!

Incidentally, I've found that trout hooked on a slack line are especially startled and angry when they feel the hook's sting, so look for a violent reaction. The 3X or heavier tippets generally employed in wet-fly work can stand a little jolt; thus the angler's strike may be quick and crisp, although there's no need to derrick the victim heavenward. With practice, you can learn to make your strikes short and sharp, moving the fly no more than a few inches and yet sufficient to set the hook, should a customer be at hand. Surely you may drive your hook into an unreachable snag, but how could you know that the drowned tree limb wasn't old Goliath? A certain amount of fly mortality is a necessary and unavoidable hazard when dead drifting down deep, and it is an acceptable one when balanced against the potential rewards.

I'm going to recount one final anecdote that emphasizes the everyday hazards of glare, most especially for the angler attempting to strike on a slack line. Two of us were fishing high on the upper Pinos River in southern Colorado at a point where the infant stream runs through a very narrow, brushy canyon. It was a bright, overcast day in late June with the water still high although quite clear, and I opted for a nymph while my partner went with floaters. He took the left bank facing up, and I the right, for we wanted to stick together in order to compare notes as we went along. It turned out that each of us had to cast quite a bit upstream and into a fierce glare in order to avoid spoiling the other's water. Several hours had passed when a call from the other bank broke my concentration: "Not our day, let's eat lunch." I didn't disagree, for we had but five trout between us. He was already out on the bank, and I waded upstream a few yards before joining him, flipping my nymph into a glide across the current along the opposite bank. It was the first time I had seen my fly all day, and to my considerable amazement, at least four trout went for the artificial almost instantly. My leader braked to a halt—I struck and was fast to a nice trout, all in about 30 seconds. It was a short lunch after that, and it soon became quite evident that the action was anything but slow, as we had supposed; indeed, nymphing was terrific and no doubt could have been all along. Thereafter, each of us worked water along the other's bank by using the "leap-frog" method. This means that I left the water on my side for him by skirting the river along the canyon wall, re-entering about 50 yards above. When he reached my re-entry point, he in turn cut around and above me, and so on. Leap-frogging is more work, but on this day, it improved our catch many, many times over. This time, we were able to bail ourselves out of a bad visibility problem by changing casting angles; but what if conditions had remained poor? For instance, on small brushy water, you may not be able to cast across stream and there are also times when glare is bad in every direction. On the Pinos, I had already established to my satisfaction that a dragged fly wouldn't work, and dry flies were getting a chilly reception, so what then? Do you go with a dead-drifted but invisible nymph that gets a lot of attention from the trout, or settle for just a few strikes on a dry fly, at least knowing that when one comes along you can see the rise? It's a difficult situation for reasons that are psychological, but I would always try to stay with the fly the trout prefer, no matter how hard it may be to hook them. It's the best possible time to sharpen your striking skills (that is) having cooperative trout under challenging conditions, and with a little extra concentration, perhaps seasoned with a bit of luck and intuition, you should eventually prosper. The dry fly can become a crutch at such times.

We hear a lot today about "execution" in athletics. Football players are graded for execution in blocking, tackling, running pass patterns, and the like, as a means of judging performance. If fly fishers were to be graded in this way, I would put alertness and concentration at the top of the list of attributes to be evaluated. When it comes to slack-line striking, execution grades for these qualities must be high if you are to win many games—no question about it. Concentration can be affected by many factors, such as fatigue, a headache, other fishermen, an impending storm, and so on, but for most of us, the biggest distraction is simply poor fishing! It's only natural to become flat and inattentive when the action is slow, and yet this is precisely when you need to work the hardest! Success in fly fishing is based in part on plain, old-fashioned effort!

STREAMERS

The streamer is a special kind of wet fly and one that makes a lot of sense from a biological standpoint. Small fish abound in every trout water, and the streamer is the traditional mimicker of the minnow. Thus, the streamer fisherman has an ever-present form of natural food to copy, and needn't search for prevalent nymphs or wait for a hatch to appear. Curiously, while some anglers are devoted to streamers, many others ignore these colorful flies altogether. For my own part, I've always liked streamers. Tempting the trout with a big minnow copy is appealing, somehow. Nonetheless, I'll bet I didn't catch a dozen trout on them during the first dozen seasons of my angling career. The problem was that although I liked the *idea* of the streamer as a trout lure and always had some in my fly book, I almost never got around to actually fishing with one. It goes without saying that a fly can't do much for you if it never gets wet, and in my case, the streamers might as well have been a collection of good-luck charms. It finally took a violent storm to convert me from a "carrier" into a "user."

Some years ago, we lived in Colorado Springs, close enough to fishing that I could make short forays to a stream in the rolling mountains northwest of mighty Pike's Peak. My favorite spot was a long meadow through which this brook snaked its way in a series of tight curves before spilling into a deep canyon. I looked forward to these little trips, but this particular day was overcast and unusually hot and muggy. I felt "flat" that morning, lacking my customary enthusiasm, and the trout apparently did too, for by noon I had elicited no more than a few half-hearted strikes. Then, in what seemed no more than a few minutes, towering blue-black clouds gathered from all sides, and ominous growls of thunder drowned out the stream's voice. It became apparent that the meadow was no place to be, and so I beat a hasty retreat into the mouth of the canyon, scrambling for shelter in a shallow cave along the face of a

cliff. I'm not especially afraid of electrical storms, but this one resembled the finale of a Fourth of July fireworks celebration and centered itself directly overhead. Crackling bolts of lightning, slicing through sheets of rain, bounced back and forth from the canyon rim above and sent me cowering to the depths of the crevice, where I remained pinned for nearly two hours. When I emerged, the stream's depth had more than doubled, and the previously warm, clear water had turned to icy, milked coffee. It was no surprise when my big dry flies were ignored. As I sloshed unhappily back to the car through drifts of hail, thoughts of worms and spinners flashed by, for I had confidently promised the neighbors a few fish for dinner. Then, one of my previously untried streamer patterns came to mind. This was an unusual fly I had purchased primarily for high-lake fishing; it was tied with fluffy, white Marabou feathers. At least the flies were big, and thinking that the white feathers might be visible through the murk, I rummaged through the more remote pockets of my jacket in search of a book reserved for "odd" flies. It was a last-ditch effort—but to this day, I haven't seen any lure or bait assaulted as violently as those trout hit that Marabou. They struck with intent to kill, whether the streamer was drifting free, racing across a current, or being dragged back against the flow. Surely, bait and lures would have worked too, but I doubt that anything could have kept pace with the marabous until the last one was virtually chewed apart. Instead of defeating me, the storm had brought the easiest fishing that I ever experienced on that brook.

Of course, I was delighted with my new ace-in-the-hole for roily water, and yet only ten weeks later, the same pattern saved me from an entirely different sort of dilemma under opposite conditions. Each fall we made a trip to the famous Fryingpan River in central Colorado; on this occasion, I had been looking forward to fishing a particular half-mile stretch that was partially hidden and a bit removed from the road. Many of us do our most successful fishing in daydreams during the off season, and this pretty piece of water had yielded hundreds of trophy trout, albeit imaginary ones.

As if specially ordered, the day was a gorgeous example of October's bright blue weather, highlighted by perfect dry-fly water. As I approached a particularly provocative canyon, my bursting anticipation was further increased by a nice Brown that came from some distance to swallow a floating Adams that I had tied with special care for the trip. However, excitement and carelessness are not strangers, and my prize Adams was soon fast to the branch of a huge spruce that spread beyond its neighbors high above the water. Irritated, I was forced to snap the leader, and while wrenching my fly box from a tight pocket, I managed to break the worn strap on my camera. As I feared, water droplets on the shutter spelled doom for this faithful piece of equipment. Trembling with anger, I put on another tippet, tied on my next-best Adams, turned back upstream, and promptly threw my backcast into the identical bough! Now both flies would rust into oblivion in tandem! At this point, I recall that certain remarks were made out loud to the innocent spruce as if it had planned the whole thing, whereupon I proceeded to put on a demonstration of how *not* to fish a dry fly. I clearly needed to cool off somehow before I shattered the rod across my knee, and once again the streamers came to mind. I had been curious to see the unusual marabou feathers in action ever since that stormy day when muddy water had pretty well hidden the fly, and watching the marabou swim about seemed like a pleasant if temporary diversion from the sour dry-fly fishing. In the interests of psychotherapy, therefore, I made the change, although with no expectation of catching anything. After all, this was prime dry-fly time on a great dry-fly stream! Thus I was surprised when a small trout followed the streamer back to my feet on a natural drift. The very next cast produced a jarring strike that I missed because I wasn't ex-

pecting it, and magically, the earlier disasters were all but forgotten. By now, I had entered the canyon where I could cast upstream at an angle into the main current, watching the fly dead drift quite deep. I spotted a glimmer of white, undulating feathers some five feet down, when suddenly another glint appeared close by, and striking by reflex, I was fast to what turned out to be the largest Rainbow I have taken from this fine river. After a prolonged battle, I emerged victorious from the canyon to find that the Fryingpan changed its character dramatically above, forming a long riffle punctuated here and there by surfacing rocks. Any thought of returning to a floating fly was soon discarded, because now I found that I could fish the streamer as if it *were* a dry fly, and with deadly effect. Lighting conditions were such that I had good visibility, and the riffled surface provided a measure of cover.

I could easily follow the pulsating bundle of white feathers after roll casts of 20 feet or so into or above holding pockets. The streamer seldom made it through the trip unscathed, however, for there were hordes of attackers just waiting to make off with it. Like all anglers, I've been through enough fishless days that I seldom feel guilty when the trout are striking wildly, but this time it almost seemed a shame to take such easy advantage.

These two experiences gave me a warm feeling for the White Marabou, because, in each case, the fly had unexpectedly turned around what started out to be a bad day. It's easy enough to understand the streamer's stunning success after the storm. Presumably, the sudden surge of water that followed washed shoal-seeking minnows along with other types of food into major currents where they became easy prey for eagerly foraging trout. It's more difficult to know why streamers sometimes do so well in situations like that on the Fryingpan. Interestingly, other anglers reported disappointing dry-fly fishing on that particular day in view of the apparently excellent conditions for floaters. It seemed that the better trout were relatively inactive in terms of surface feeding, preferring to stay close to their holding water, as the big Rainbow that I took from the bottom of the channel current had done. It may be that on such days smaller trout grow bolder and become more active themselves, thereby enhancing the value of a fly that copies a minnow. Similarly, there are those exciting occasions on streams and lakes alike when the trout tend to run large, with few little fellows making an appearance. Perhaps when the big boys are out and about, small fry find it prudent to stick close to home.

In any event, for a time, I really thought the white Marabou feathers had supernatural powers. Marabou fluffs were once best known as the functional part of fan-dancers' fans (back in those days when they used fans). I found the undulating strand of wetted feather to be as provocative to trout as Marabou fluffs must have been to customers of old-time burlesque houses. However, my infatuation with Marabous was eventually tempered by an experience on the Big Wood River below Magic Dam in southern Idaho. It was mid-October, and the outflow had been reduced to a trickle of seepage just sufficient to keep deep potholes fresh along an otherwise dry canyon bed below the lava-strewn desert floor. The Marabou's first journey through one of the pools attracted a veritable flotilla of a dozen or more trout, flanking the fly in the manner of a convoy escort. Still more intriguing, these fish ran from large to larger to unbelievable! My hands shook so hard that the Marabou acquired a novel sort of jiggle during the retrieve, but regardless of this seductive shimmy, the Rainbows did no more than make tantalizing passes, coming within inches of the fly. It was a weird experience, for I knew there had to be a better way to go after these beauties, and yet I simply couldn't tear myself away from the teasing performance the Marabou put on in one hole after another. It was I who was hooked! By evening, my catch amounted to a pair of relatively puny 12-inchers. Of course I was back the next morning, this time having sworn off the Marabous in favor of less flashy streamers. Although the more se-

date flies attracted almost no visible interest, they produced a slow, steady flow of solid strikes throughout the day, and I hooked a total of 11 fish; eight of these were better than 14 inches, with one in the monster class. On that trip, I learned that a fly can be fantastically exciting to trout without provoking serious strikes, just as in the case of a dry fly with a high strike/hook ratio. As to the Fryingpan, subsequent trials with the marvelous Marabou were successful, although never again producing the remarkable fishing I enjoyed on that first autumn day of dry-fly frustration.

During the seasons that followed, I began to experiment with some of the more "drab" streamer patterns such as the Muddler Minnow, bucktails tied with hair wings, and Marabous utilizing dyed grey, brown, or black feathers. As on the Wood River, I found that these patterns sometimes enjoyed a better credibility rating than did the scintillating White Marabou.

The next step in my evolution as a streamer fisherman involved learning some lessons about methods of presentation. There are several ways in which these flies may be displayed in front of the trout. The most classical is probably the current swing described earlier wherein the fly is brought more or less across the direction of flow. This sort of behavior would hardly be possible for a lifeless or feebly swimming creature, hence the cross-current maneuver creates the kind of activity one might expect from a minnow. The drag retrieve against the current is based on the same logic. In relatively quiet water, it's necessary to give a streamer at least a little life-like swimming movement, and as in the case of cross-current and upstream drags, an angler has almost unlimited opportunity for variation in speed and steadiness of retrieval and in fly depth. Finally, there's the natural drift. This method had come through so nicely for me on the Fryingpan that several seasons later I nearly missed some fine fishing by depending too much on dead drifts. Wild Horse Creek's setting in the rugged Pioneer Mountains east of Sun Valley, Idaho, is as picturesque as its name, and on the July morning in question, I was delighted to find a hatch of May flies already in progress. The water was a bit high and cold, although clear enough to suggest a probable bonanza with dry flies. Nonetheless, the trout were not about to rise to the naturals, let alone to my attempts at imitation, and soon the hatch was over. Having no better plan, I went to a White Marabou fished upstream and natural drift, but still there were no takers. Finally, I came to a deep current that stood out from rather shoal surroundings in a most inviting manner. This water was far prettier than any I had come upon, and I carefully positioned myself on a gravel bar for a quartering and upstream cast above the heart of my target. From this vantage point I could get a 60-foot float right down the pike before the channel turned at a 45 degree angle, losing depth to become a riffle. It was a simple matter to lob the fly upstream on a slack line, allow it to sink to a selected depth and dead drift to the end of its tether at the bend. It was such an altogether compelling

piece of water that I hardly noticed the deep eddy almost in my shadow to the left. In fact, at the completion of the first few floats, I allowed the fly to wash down the riffle rather than fishing the eddy at all. Finally, since the eddy was in the direct line of my retrieve, I crawled the Marabou back slowly through its still depths as a matter of habit. To my annoyance, the submarining streamer hung up. There was no tug, the fly just came to a halt as it would against a snag. I gave the Marabou a gentle jerk in an effort to free it and was eventually successful—although I had to chase a 16-inch, spade-shaped Rainbow all over Wild Horse Creek first! In any sort of competitive sport, when you find one or another tactic that seems to work, it makes sense to go back to it, and on this morning I set out to find similar pieces of deep slack. As it turned out, the streamer was totally ineffective when dead drifted, swung across current, or retrieved rapidly in any kind of water, but it almost never failed to produce

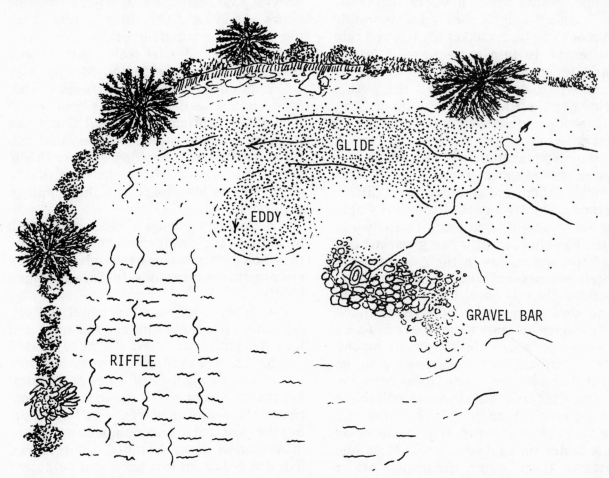

when fished slowly and well sunken in deep slack. The real problem was finding enough of the right kind of water until, toward 4:00 p.m., another hatch of duns came along, this time bringing a good rise with it. Significantly, while I eventually took more trout that day on dry flies, all of the large ones were caught on the Marabou!

Most streamer advocates prefer to introduce a certain amount of unevenness into their retrieves, either through a series of rod-tip twitches, or by means of the left hand, as in Ray Bergman's well-known "Hand Twist Retrieve." Here the left thumb and forefinger grasp the line below the last guide with the palm up. By turning the hand over briskly, three or four inches of line are brought in. Now the fourth and fifth fingers hook themselves over the line below the guide, at the same time releasing the thumb-finger hold. By returning the hand to its original palm-up position, another short length of line is pulled in, and the process is then repeated by allowing the line to slide off the lower fingers while regaining a thumb-finger hold. This simple sequence can be cycled at the desired rate and tempo to impart a slight although realistic irregularity to the retrieve. Perhaps it's not fair to call the action created by the Hand Twist "realistic," but at least it's widely used and obviously effective.

Which presentation is best then? The answer is the same as for any wet fly, that is, none of them and all of them—at different times. There's no need to buy any single method as superior; indeed, it's foolish to do so. The kind of water being worked can limit the options, as in the case of slack targets where some kind of added action is desirable. In this case, I strongly recommend slow retrieves as opposed to quick darting ones, at least to begin with. There seems to be a definite consensus among veteran lure and fly fishermen alike to the effect that a leisurely swimming retrieve, perhaps a bit jerky but still *slow*, will beat a fast one much of the time. In this context, I like to work pockets of minnow-infested slack water up against a bank. Here one may cast from center stream against or

even onto the bank before subtly twitching the streamer out into target water. Alternatively, it's sometimes even better to stand on the bank, cast onto the central current, and then ease the fly gently back into the slack in the manner of a minnow seeking refuge. With the understanding that there is no best presentation, I must still rate a natural drift as the most generally productive method. You might think that a drifting streamer would just tumble along rather than "streaming" properly in the current, minnow style, but trout don't seem to see this as a problem. Trial and error have taught me to give the natural drift the first shot, even as on Wild Horse Creek, for there's always plenty of time to try the various drag options.

I've attempted to summarize those situations that suggest possible success with streamers (although not necessarily in order of importance).

1. Post-storm roil. Streamers have come to my rescue time and again, usually proving most effective during the first few hours of high and (or) dirty water. Later, the supply of runoff-liberated easy food probably dwindles as trout appetite and feeding activity subside accordingly.

2. High, cold water of early season before surface feeding becomes a factor. A lure fisherman once remarked that I use streamers in the same situations that call for spinners and spoons in his book. This is likely true, especially in the case of the showy White Marabous with their built-in shimmy action.

3. After or during a wind storm, with or without high water and roil. It may be that food gets blown into the water, thereby encouraging minnows to forage more boldly.

4. When conditions are right for dry flies in your estimation, but the trout are less than enthusiastic. What's there to lose?

5. When "headhunting" or going after larger fish, regardless of water conditions. My records show that a surprising proportion of the really good trout I've taken during the past decade succumbed to the lure of a minnow copy. As noted before, large fish don't rise without good and sufficient

reason, and while high interest hatches aren't common on most waters, minnows are around throughout the season. For that matter, a streamer may capture some nice trout in the very midst of a hatch and rise! Cannibalistic trout are not above turning their attentions to a foolish minnow that attempts to compete for surface food. (Under these circumstances, rapid jerky retrieves just beneath the surface can pay off.)

When it comes to specific streamer patterns, there is considerable wisdom in consulting local anglers, for regional favorites are likely to have earned their reputations. Beyond this, the famous Muddler Minnow is a nearly universal choice among streamer advocates today, and it would probably win an overall popularity poll hands down. I give the Muddler (or some variant thereof) and the White Marabou about equal emphasis in my own fishing, although these two patterns are about 180 degrees apart in most respects. The Muddler's large head of shaped deer hair and prominent feather wing give the fly a thick, blocky silhouette in contrast to the slender, pencil-like Marabou. The Muddler's hair hackle and stiff wing are much more rigid than the supple strand of Marabou feather, for the latter literally "breathes" in the water. Aside from a thin tinsel body, largely covered by hackle, the Muddler is a rather drab brown-grey creation in comparison with the sore-thumb flash of the white Marabou feather. In fact, these patterns are so different that I often fish one against the other in an attempt to discover the trout's preference, and they often have one, too. Some of the Muddler's fine reputation may have to do with its ability to mimic food forms other than minnows. In the surface film, it makes a convincing grasshopper; deeper, it may suggest a thick-bodied nymph. In any event, it has proven to be an excellent partner in contrasts for the Marabou. I'll never forget an August day in 1975 when Muddlers caught *eight times* as many trout as did the White Marabous on Wyoming's broad Hoback River, southeast of Jackson. I fished each pattern for exactly three hours,

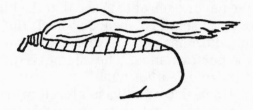

MARABOU STREAMER

MUDDLER MINNOW

and the Muddler concluded its performance by taking a chunky, three-pound Cutthroat! Naturally, when the white fly combines its attractor qualities with solid strikes, it's tough to beat. I frequently give the Marabou the first shot if for no other reason than that I can see it better than darker patterns. As on the Fryingpan, when fly visibility is reasonably good, a streamer presented dead drift and near the top is very much like fishing a dry fly, since the trout's approach and take are evident. This makes for exciting sport. Popular hybrid flies combine the Muddler's hair head with the Marabou's wing, although I really prefer the fully contrasting patterns. There are innumerable other streamer patterns. The older, traditional ones can be quite fancy and complicated, virtual works of art, combining different feathers; some of them are brilliantly colored, with tinsel, hair, painted eyes, and so on. The simpler bucktails feature streaming bundles of hair, and there are all manner of new synthetic materials for streamer wings as well. In any event, I believe that the sinuous minnow form and action count far more than do tiny details of construction. In the case of Marabous, for example, I have never been able to see that the kind of body (tinsel, floss, peacock herl, fur dubbing, etc.) has any effect whatever on the fly's performance. The magic is in that tantalizing feather wing!

Hook size usually isn't terribly critical in streamer fishing, because the trailing wing makes for a substantial silhouette anyway, and streamer hooks are 3 or 4X long shanked to begin with. Thus, even a small-caliber streamer doesn't look particularly delicate as it swims along because of its long wheelbase. I use streamers as small as no. 16s on occasion, but I depend for the most part on 6s, 8s, and 10s. As explained in the next chapter, hook size has a lot to do with fly weight, and I usually make my choice on the basis of the weight I want. Incidentally, I don't worry a great deal about using a streamer that's too large, for trout will take on flies (and minnows too) that nearly rival them in size. In the big waters of the Rio Grande's box canyon in northern New Mexico, I'll go with streamers so large that they would be keepers if they were real fish. The legendary Browns of "the Box" are hardly intimidated by no. 4 hooks!

In summary, I've found that streamers may produce handsomely in almost any setting and at any time, regardless of the season, weather, water conditions, and so on. Clearly, the streamer deserves its traditional niche among trout flies, whether as a regular weapon in one's armamentarium, or on an ace-in-the-hole basis. The important thing is to get these big, colorful flies out of your hatband and into the water where they can show their stuff!

WEIGHTED WET FLIES

The trouble with poking fun at bait fishermen is that some of them catch so many trout, and big ones at that! These are not the kind of folk who warm the top of a favorite rock all day, but active anglers who wade up the stream, read the water, dead drift their baits, slack-line strike, and so on. They attack a stream aggressively in the finest fly-fishing tradition. In fact, it might be more honest to turn the tradition part around, for I suspect that historically the expert bait fishers came first. In any event, I admire many of their techniques and have no hesitation whatever in applying them to fly fishing. For instance, a major cornerstone in the foundation of their philosophy is to "get the bait *down*." It seems that as a general rule, bottom baits are more likely to be taken than are those fished near the surface or only halfway down. It is probably significant that most successful spin fishers of my acquaintance also prefer to bump their deep-running spoons and spinners off the bottom. I'm quite certain the same is true for wet flies, so while the "deep is good" idea probably goes way back in history, the concept bears repeating, no matter what you're fishing with.

Unlike a large spoon or glob of worms, a fly has little weight of its own, and so in deep or fast water, some modification of the terminal tackle is required if the artificial is to get down where the action is. There are three ways in which this may be accomplished: (1) a sinking line, (2) weighting the leader (as with split shot), and (3) weighting the fly itself. In comparing these methods, one needs to consider several features about the stream he is fishing. The most obvious is target depth; how far down is down? Secondly, there is the question of "time." How much time does the fly have to reach the desired depth? Here there are two separate factors, float distance and current speed. In other words, how far above the target is it possible or practical to cast the fly, and how long will the fly take to float down to its destination? If your cast can be aimed well above the target and into slow water, the fly should have plenty of time to reach the desired depth. On the other hand, if it has to be dropped just above or even into the target zone, especially in a swift current, time is going to be short. And when it comes to simple drag retrieves, current speed directly influences fly depth; the swifter the current, the higher in the water it will want to ride. As you can see, tackle adjustments to meet variable stream situations are critical.

Taking the options in order, you will find that sinking lines need a lot of time in order to do their job effectively. This is because they have to get down themselves before they can influence the leader and fly. As a consequence, sinking lines are of little help when the fly has to be thrown close to its target. I use them primarily on big water where long, unobstructed floats are possible. Of course, sinking lines are perfect for slow-moving rivers, ponds, and lakes, but even in these circumstances, I sometimes look for another alternative when short casts are advantageous or when a floating line tip helps me detect strikes.

Split shot will certainly do the job, although I find this to be an awkward solution. If the shot is placed high on the leader, for instance above the tippet splice knot some 18 inches from the end, your fly may ride high in the current while the shot probes along the bottom instead. Additionally, accurate casts are difficult with the fly-split-shot tandem since it is the shot that tends to hit your target rather than the fly.

For these reasons, I began to experiment with weighted wets a number of years ago, despite the fact that they were (and still are) somewhat unorthodox. They have a bad "press," based on the notion that the added weight makes them sluggish, dead acting, and unresponsive to minor currents. It's perfectly true that if enough solder, lead wire, or whatever is applied to a hook, it can be made to plummet to the bottom in the manner of an anchor. Your best chance with this kind of fly is to hit the fish over the head and stun them, but weighting is a quantitative thing, and we are talking about rather small quantities of lead wire wrapped under the body construction materials. Heavy-gauge hooks designed for wet flies sink to an extent by themselves, especially in the larger calibers. However, just a little added lead wire can make a big difference, and I must say that in my own experience, the trout haven't been the least offended by this degree of weighting. A check of my log book for the past five seasons shows that the great majority of the trout I've taken on sunken flies were hooked on weighted wets.

There's no question that weighted flies are becoming more popular, although unfortunately, they are still hard to find on the usual tackle counter and may have to be ordered specially at extra cost. Here the angler who ties his own flies is in great shape, because weighting hooks is both easy and inexpensive. Moreover, it is possible to vary the weights of a whole series of nymphs, streamers, or whatever so that you may select the perfect fly for a particular stream or even a stretch of special water. Ever-changing depth, current speed, and size of targets usually call for specific fly weights. Thus I carry individual patterns in two or three different weights on the *same* size hook as follows:

1. Unweighted.

2. Minimally weighted (a strip or two of small-diameter lead wire tied on parallel to the hook shaft beneath the body).

3. Lightly weighted (fine or medium lead wire wrapped around the hook shaft under body-construction materials).

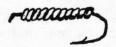

A 200-yard stretch of the Brazos River in northern New Mexico comes to mind as an example of water that requires three separate fly weights if it is to be worked in optimal fashion. Let's assume that I'm fishing with a good-sized nymph, say a no. 10, presenting it deep and bumping bottom. The lower end of this segment is wide and shoal, featuring a long, slow glide toward the center of the channel. This glide is only about 18 inches deep and can be worked systematically via quartering and upstream casts of 30 feet or so. Here an unweighted fly is ideal, reaching bottom within a few feet of its entry point. Just upstream, however, the channel pinches in to form a powerful, six-foot-deep current. Beneath the surface rip, one can barely make out jagged rocks resembling a miniature submerged mountain range, and between these mossy crags lurk some trout that any angler might covet. The flow is so strong that even a fully weighted nymph needs 15 feet of float in order to probe the bottom. I must cast well upstream each time as I slowly work toward the head of the channel. Just above, the river splits around an island in an area where the surface is broken by numerous boulders. The current is generally swift, and the pockets or windows of holding water below each rock are roughly 2½ feet in depth. Here the relatively heavy nymph I needed minutes before in the deep channel sinks quickly in sullen, lifeless fashion, hanging up on the bottom before it can pass through these pockets. Going back to the unweighted nymph that floated so naturally down the glide is no solution either, for there is still enough current to carry this fly out of the pockets before it can sink more than a few inches. But now a lightly weighted nymph is "just right." The trick is to lob the fly directly on top of the rock and twitch it off gently so that the current eases it along the intimate contours of the bottom. In summary, I fish this segment of river with the same pattern and hook size throughout, and yet I change flies at least twice! Certainly it's a bother to juggle hook weights, but almost any amount of extra trouble is worthwhile if the reward is a more effective presentation, and in this regard, fly depth is frequently critical. I don't wish to convey the idea that one needs to adjust fly weight to conform to each little wrinkle in target depth or current that comes along; this would be foolish. Very often a single fly will do pretty well for the great majority of water in a given stream.

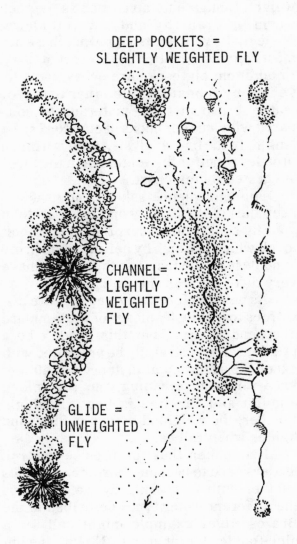

DEEP POCKETS =
SLIGHTLY WEIGHTED FLY

CHANNEL=
LIGHTLY
WEIGHTED
FLY

GLIDE =
UNWEIGHTED
FLY

There are seasonal variations in weight selection too. Early in the season, we expect to encounter deeper, swifter water, and it is then that the heavier flies are most useful. Of course, the prime factor in determining how much ballast, if any, a fly needs has to do with the water level at which the trout are feeding. If they are performing up topside, as in taking May fly nymphs about to hatch, it would be silly to go with a weighted fly at all. It's a very different matter when the fly's mission is to copy larvae such as those of the Crane fly or Stone fly that tend to bump along the bottom.

Predicting the best probable feeding depth can be difficult, and it is sometimes amazing how much trout reaction to a fly is influenced by minor differences in ballast. An incident that took place on the North Platte River in Wyoming is a good example. It was late August, and dry-fly time was at hand, thanks to a steady profusion of May fly hatches beginning each afternoon toward 4:00 p.m. One morning we got started well ahead of the expected rise, while the Platte was still sound asleep. Several hours of exercise with floating flies produced nothing beyond bursitis in my casting elbow, and so we headed for the bank and some lunch. The usual picnic ants joined us in the shade of a bushy juniper, but these were no ordinary beasts. Almost an inch long, the shiny black fellows crawled boldly into a sack of potato chips, carrying off large pieces like umbrellas. We ate slowly, vainly watching the river for signs of surface feeding while the ants scavanged our remaining crumbs. All remained quiet, and in hopes of resting my elbow for the evening's activities, I decided to begin the afternoon with a black ant wet fly. My thoughts were really focused several hours into the future toward the dry-fly excitement to come, and I saw the ant merely as an easy way to pass the time. This fly is the absolute ultimate in simplicity, for its composition involves nothing more than a hook, black thread, lacquer, and a few hair fibers to simulate legs. The ant depends in part on its silhouette for success, since the fat abdomen is separated from a smaller thorax by a short gap of bare hook, thus creating a wasp-waist (or better, ant-waist) profile. Multiple coats of lacquer give the surface a life-like, glossy grey sheen. I ordinarily preferred an unweighted no. 12 hook for this ant, since the real insect would likely remain close to the surface, but I had tied a couple utilizing short wraps of lead wire to build up the abdomen and thorax lumps, later covering them with thread. In this area, south of Encampment, the Platte is a canyon river boasting big, tough water broken by occasional boulders. I intended to concentrate on the bank water, because it seemed reasonable that our luncheon visitors and their friends would be found there; however, a large rock pocket just opposite in mid-river looked too good to pass up. Tying on my largest ant, a lightly weighted no. 10, I fought my way out through buffeting currents, anchored my feet as best I could, and fired the fly well above the boulder. Gathering currents swept the little ant deep along the rock's face no more than ten feet in front of me, when suddenly my leader jumped backward a full six inches, and I was fast to a 15-inch Rainbow. The hour that followed won't soon be forgotten, for while I captured only a half-dozen trout; all were large, all took quite deep (two feet or more) and all struck with zeal. Most of the hour was spent pursuing angry fish downriver, until I struck too hard against an enormous (?) Rainbow, and the tippet parted. With him went the second and last of my weighted ants, together with all of the excitement. It goes without saying that I turned at once to an unweighted no. 12 ant, but disappointingly, I simply couldn't get it down more than a foot in the surging currents despite a stout sinking line. After 20 minutes, it hadn't elicited a single strike, and the gentle bank water also proved sterile. A weighted no. 10 Martinez Black sunk nicely to the desired depth, but on this day at least, it lacked the ant's magic, taking only two smallish trout in the next hour. Of course, this was hardly a well-controlled experiment; few angling experiences are. I have no way to prove that the trout didn't just stop hitting at the very instant that I lost my last weighted ant. Nonetheless, it's

interesting that each of the several trout I killed had one or more of the monster ants in its stomach. (How they got into the deep currents at mid-river remains a mystery.)

Fly weight is determined by a number of factors other than added lead. Big hooks, particularly the heavy-gauge, long-shanked kind with which large nymphs and streamers are tied, have a lot of intrinsic weight. Elongate nymphs such as the rock worm or Crane fly and the well-known Stone fly larva with its long wheelbase are most convincingly tied on this sort of hook. In addition, big hooks are necessarily covered by considerable quantities of water-absorbent tying materials as compared with smaller hooks of standard shaft length. In the final analysis, there is a much broader range of fly weights than the three suggested by my chart.

For convenience' sake, it's advisable to keep flies of different weights separate in your fly book. I find it surprisingly difficult to tell which is which by hefting them in my hand despite the fact that they will behave very differently in the water.

As noted before, weighted flies are disastrous to handle by means of the standard overhead fly cast, but this needn't be a problem. They can easily be presented with excellent accuracy at distances of 40 feet via a roll cast, providing your rod is long enough and the line is heavy enough. Further, the weighted fly is a potent wind fighter when roll cast.

Remember that for precise control, leaders need to become shorter and tippets heavier with increasing fly weight. Thus the different water types described in the Brazos River example might call for a nine-foot leader tapered to 3X with the unweighted nymph, a stubby six-footer tapered to 1X for the heavy nymph fished deep in the strong channel rip, and a 7½-footer tapered to 2X in the pocket water above. The latter leader-tippet combination has a wide range of usefulness and will do the job nicely throughout much of an average day with wet flies. Therefore, leader manipulations needn't become a major chore, although they are important when needed to improve casting accuracy.

Many anglers worry that the splash a weighted fly makes on entry will frighten their quarry; however, I have found this disturbance to be more of a plus than a minus on many occasions. Possibly mistaking the splash for the rise of a small fish, trout sometimes smack the fly a split second after it hits. Perhaps in the case of a streamer, they go after the "minnow" they think might have made the commotion. The splash of a nymph could suggest the missed rise of another trout—who knows? In any event, I've failed to hook a good many trout when taken by surprise in this way. It's hard to gain control of the slack so quickly after your cast.

To sum up, in my experience, those anglers who use flies that are weighted *just enough* to get them down where the fish are taking have been uniformly enthusiastic about weighted wets. These once maligned flies are invaluable allies, so long as one is careful to use as little ballast as necessary to get the job done! This brings us logically to the chapter on fly tying because, at least at present, weighted flies are easier to tie than to buy.

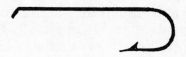

LONG SHANK & HEAVY GAUGE (WET FLY)

REGULAR SHANK (WET FLY)

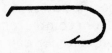

REGULAR SHANK & DRY FLY GAUGE

SAME CALIBER HOOK BUT DIFFERENT WEIGHTS !

TYING YOUR OWN

I used to think of fly tying as a nice fussy sort of hobby, something akin to building ships in bottles and reserved for elderly gentlemen. When I finally began to tie my own flies, it was neither as a hobby nor because I particularly wanted to. Ernie Schweibert's book, *Matching the Hatch*, was responsible, for as I became sold on the concept of precise mimicry, I found that most of the specific patterns I needed were not available from commercial sources. Of course, a hatch matcher can special-order such flies; however, this is expensive and inconvenient, too, unless you happen to have a professional tier sitting around waiting for your next order. Thus, I felt compelled to learn the art. My progress was slow, since I had no one to coach me, but as my creations gradually improved over the seasons, I realized that fly tying was actually helping me to become a better fisherman! I'm sure the idea that learning to tie flies makes one a more effective angler requires some explanation, and accordingly, this chapter is devoted not to the hows of fly tying, but to the whys.

In these days of one-dollar flies, it's hard to dispute the simple argument that one saves money. Nonetheless, I really think there are even better reasons for tying your own. If you look at a commercial venture, either a factory setup or a single tier's operation, it becomes clear that the cost of each fly has relatively little to do with construction materials. *Tier time* is the real cost factor, since the finest professionals can turn out only so many units per hour. This is tedious work too, in any kind of volume, and so most tiers are essentially paid on a piecework basis. It follows that commercial assembly-line fly tying must stress quantity over quality. However, when you put together a fly for your own use, tying time becomes free, in a sense, and the quantity versus quality relationship tends to reverse itself. This brings up an obvious and practical question: just how

hard is it to tie really good flies? The fact of the matter is that fly fabrication is more of a knack than a super skill, and people with rather limited manual dexterity can still turn out highly effective flies. I've taught enough beginners to be sure that this is so, provided that they work at it and constantly try to improve. Reasonable nymphs and streamers should roll out of the vise after a few hours of practice, and while top-quality dry flies require a bit more skill, some of the most effective patterns are also the simplest to tie. The point of all this is very blunt. With a little time and effort, you will soon be able to tie *better* flies than you can buy in the usual tackle shop! Admittedly, there are individual commercial tiers who create impeccable flies that are sold privately or through quality outlets. I once spent several hours pawing through hundreds of hair-winged dry flies in the bins of a famous tackle emporium in Manhattan, and by selecting the very best, I came away with three dozen superb artificials. This was at a time when good hair wings were beyond my own tying skills, but what if my order had come by mail to be filled by a clerk? You can be sure that while the patterns and sizes would have been the same, the individual flies would not, for even in this mecca, there was considerable variation in quality.

Fly quality is not simply a matter of the care taken in construction, either. For instance, hackle is the most vital part of a dry fly's anatomy, and hackle feathers come in different grades from the expensive, stiff fibered kind that float a fly so well to softer, less desirable feathers. As an individual tying for my own needs, I can well afford to discard any mediocre hackle, while someone who must cost account his materials is naturally reluctant to cull usable hackle, even if it is second rate.

This brings us to individual preferences in fly construction, a closely related issue. Some anglers prefer dry flies with slightly long, sparse hackles, while others like thick hackles, a bit on the short side. The first fly is ideal for quiet, glassy surfaces, while the second will float better in swift, broken water. Some like dry flies with long, slender tails; others opt for short, brushy tails, and there are several choices pertaining to body and wing construction as well. Hence the angler who ties his own is assured of having just the kind of fly he wants, whatever the occasion. These construction variables are understandably hard to control through the mail or even across the counter.

Then there is the occasional opportunity to tie an exquisitely precise pattern to match an important hatch. I was once lucky enough to be on Idaho's famed Silver Creek for five consecutive days during a magnificent hatch of small, dark May fly duns. This hatch was highly predictable, beginning about 8:30 a.m. and lasting for approximately 75 minutes. Having identified the insect as to genus and species on the first day, I came back the next morning prepared with several good-looking matching patterns in the exact size. However, though they were convincing to *my* eye, Silver Creek's big Rainbows saw my creation quite differently. They persistently took naturals floating only inches from my fly, capsizing it in the wake of their rise, for added insult. Each morning I returned, full of hope, with a newly modified pattern, only to go through

another exercise in frustration. When a hatch is truly blizzard-like, as this one was, and the rise is really massive, one's ego tends to suffer. I just couldn't seem to find the right hackle shade, until I got a crazy idea, born of desperation, on the evening before the last fishing day. Putting aside my collection of black, grizzly, blue and grey dun feathers, I rubbed greasy soot from the inside of our cabin chimney onto pure white hackle until it resembled the dark-mottled naturals I had preserved. The resulting fly was pretty awful from a cosmetic standpoint; however, on the following morning, my dirty "chimney sweep" fly did a great job for me, hooking a dozen Rainbows, and keeping the line taut throughout the entire hatch. Now there was a different kind of frustration when a mere 12-incher took my fly, since every fish had to be played carefully on fine tippets, and there were much bigger quarry at stake. There are many who know Silver Creek's difficult hatches better than I, but the other anglers with whom I shared that particular hatch were all having a fairly rough time of it, and so I was rather proud of my sooty fly.

The need to imitate a natural food form isn't always restricted to dainty flies, and on several occasions, I've run into bulky insects that were hard to copy. The enormous flying ant is one of them. Reddish-brown and fully an inch in length, these fellows are among nature's worst fliers. They seem to land where the breeze takes

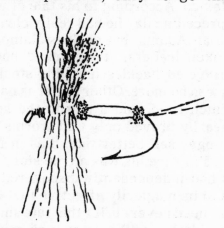

Long, sparse hackle tail

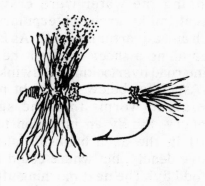

Short, heavy hackle tail

SAME PATTERN & HOOK SIZE BUT VERY DIFFERENT FLIES

them like so many leaves, long transparent wings akimbo. When numbers of flying ants are unfortunate enough to come down in the water, they create an absolute feeding craze. I have never seen a commercial matching pattern. However, it's no trick to tie an effective imitation on a large, long-shanked hook that utilizes a buoyant body of shaped deer hair and scanty hackle, flaring to the sides. A need for an unusual artificial is just as likely to involve a wet fly. I had fun with this sort of challenge on Hunter Creek, a fair-sized tributary of Colorado's Roaring Fork River that enters in the very shadow of the Aspen hospital's fracture ward. Although I was in town for summer teaching, I saw no compelling reason to shun the many nearby trout streams. Unfortunately, pickings were slim, for it was late June, and the major waters were still quite swollen by a record runoff. Hence I turned to the lower meadows of Hunter Creek. This stream's headwaters lie in the relatively gentle Williams Mountains east of Aspen and north of the loftier peaks of the Elk Range, favored by skiers and climbers. Even here, the water was so high and swift that we were forced out of the stream channel and into dense willow thickets along the banks. I took a few fat Brookies, but it was slow going, and I came away the first evening knowing that I should have done much better, for there was a prevalent insect that I could not copy with any of my flies. Specifically, the young willow fronds overhanging the water were crawling with bright, milky green caterpillars about an inch and a quarter in length. As I inched my jeep along a sheer shelf on the Smuggler Mine road overlooking the twinkling lights of Aspen far below, I thought more about the green worms than the spectacular scenery. Surely an imitation fished dead drift in the deep bankside slack should prove deadly, but where could I find such an odd fly? The next morning after class, I started to leave the office in search of some green floss or yarn when I saw something that made me reach for my portable fly-tying kit instead. The plastic liner in the trash can! It was a perfect shade. By the

time class resumed, I had tied three imitations that looked pretty good, and by dark, Hunter Creek's Brookies convinced me that my "trash" flies were better than good! I used a no. 8, 3X long-shanked hook, lightly weighted and covered by pale yellow yarn. Over this I simply tied a cape of the green plastic, wrapping it down with wide-spaced loops of green thread to imitate body segmentation. The edges of the plastic cape didn't quite meet on the fly's underside, so that the free edges tended to flare between the thread wraps, simulating stubby legs. The overall size, shape, color, slight translucency, and even the soft skin-like surface of the artifical were amazingly life-like; at least it whipped every other fly in my books by a wide margin.

Thus it was that both the delicate no. 18 "soot fly" and the crude caterpillar helped me to take trout that likely would have gone uncaught otherwise. I also got quite a kick out of improvising successful patterns from very ordinary if unusual materials (and at almost no cost)!

A very tangible payoff is the fly tier's freedom from worry about running out of a killing pattern, just when action is hottest. In this regard, I recall a long-faced fellow I once met on the Brazos River in northern New Mexico. According to his tale of woe, on the preceding day he had really cleaned up with an Adams, but zealous Rainbows had broken leaders, straightened hooks, and unraveled hackles until his stock of Adams was no more. Other patterns hadn't been much good, and a trip to the small town nearby proved only that worms and salmon eggs sell better than flies in New Mexico. I'm sure his was a true story, for we too had independently discovered the Adams to be magically effective that day. Fly tiers need never suffer this fate since a small tackle box will hold enough raw ingredients for literally dozens of wet- and dry-fly patterns. It is quite common for a shortage of a particular pattern in a particular size to develop during a trip of several days duration, a situation that is easily corrected by an hour or two at the tying vise. In fact, I do about 30 percent of my tying during an average season on an emergency basis of this sort. It is additionally rewarding to know that the flies you're tying are probably going to take trout for you within a few hours!

Apart from occasional innovative imitations such as those I've described, I'm not sure how realistic it is to expect to become the inventor of a devastating new pattern. The famous flies are not that numerous, and they took many years to evolve, but it's fun to try now and then. For instance, I noticed that the Royal Wulff or hair-winged Royal Coachman occasionally registered a higher strike/hook ratio than I liked, even in the smaller sizes. It occurred to me that the stark white wing might be responsible, and yet I wasn't anxious to sacrifice the excellent visibility the wings give to this pattern. Therefore, over a number of seasons I fooled around with lightly dyed, off-white hair wings in greys, blues, greens (and even pinks) in an effort to tone down the bright white a bit. My experiments were disappointing, for the flies were either hard to see, unattractive to the fish, or both. Finally, I stumbled onto the idea of a light gold wing, and this proved to be a minor breakthrough. The gold-winged flies stood out from flecks of foam even better than those with white wings and yet often attracted more solid strikes than the identical pattern tied with a white wing.

The rear cuff of peacock herl on the Royal's body has a way of tearing apart after taking a few fish, and so I switched to a more durable body of gold tinsel matching the gold-hair wing, but I retained the same brown hackle as in the original Royal. This pattern seemed to excite the trout, and since I developed it while fishing streams with colorful New Mexican names, I dubbed it the "Spanish Fly."

Whether you save money by tying your own depends on how much fishing you do. The initial outlay for equipment and materials isn't small, or shouldn't be, because cheap kits are liable to discourage a begin-

ner. A good vise is critical, and that alone will run $12 to $30, although a quality tool is always worth the price. My fly vise is now in its 32nd season, and shows no sign of appreciable wear. Good scissors, hackle pliers, and a fair assortment of hooks, thread, fur, feathers, and the like can easily add up to another $30, and so we are talking in terms of nearly $50 for a solid beginning. But remember that tier time is where the savings lie, and there is no sense in skimping on either equipment or materials. I tie about 20 dozen artificials each season, using the very best of everything I can buy, and the cost accounting still works out to less than $.10 per fly. Since I use, lose, or give away almost all of each year's production, I end up saving roughly $150 per annum. (This is one way to justify the purchase of an expensive rod to your wife; at least it's worth a try.)

Although many good books on fly tying are available, I've found there is no substitute for a little personal help from an accomplished tier. Watching a tier actually manipulate the materials makes up for thousands of words, many pictures and saves countless hours by helping to abort the creation of well-intentioned but poorly conceived flies. I've found that smaller sizes, say no. 18s on down, are highly intimidating to new tiers, yet someone with experience can make them look easy, and they really are. Fly tying, like fly casting, is not nearly so difficult as you might think.

To summarize, the bonuses involved in tying your own flies look something like this:

1. Better quality flies than you can generally buy.

2. An unlimited selection of patterns and sizes.

3. Control over variables of construction to fit your preferences.

4. Ability to copy natural food forms, especially when standard patterns fail.

5. "Instant" replacement of shortages created by demand.

6. Intangibles, such as creative satisfaction (particularly when your flies catch fish).

7. Very tangible money savings.

THE FINAL CAPTURE

Getting pan-sizers landed is pretty much of an academic exercise, assuming the hook has a decent hold. They simply haven't the muscle to put up much resistance. In fact, if the hook is set too hard, a little fellow is likely to land in a tree, somewhere to the rear, dangling like a Christmas ornament. Of course, it isn't a good idea to send even the smallest fish rocketing skyward. Apart from accidentally dashing the victim to death on a rock, the sudden strain may tear out the hook or snap the leader. According to tradition, one should "play" a trout, cat-and-mouse style, before landing him. Surely, youngsters like to feel a trout tug against the rod, but the notion of playing with a poor fish seems a bit foolish. "Fighting" is a more sporting term for this sort of thing, although a fight should involve some kind of exchange, and in this case the trout has a lot more to lose than does the angler, unless the latter happens to fall in during the proceedings. It's like saying that a hunter goes off with his high-powered rifle to fight the deer!

However, if the quarry is in the 12-inch range or larger, under certain conditions, it's the angler who has the short end of things. Trout commonly employ several tactics which have a very good chance of literally getting them off the hook, and as a consequence, the angler needs to make certain countermoves to forestall these tactics. In this context, the ensuing activities on the part of each party do resemble a battle of sorts, for strength and strategy are both involved.

Understanding that the trout's motives and actions are instinctive, it should follow that his basic battle plan is a simple and direct one. He "wants" to pull as hard as he can against the terminal tackle; that's all there is to it. Of course, this makes primitive sense if the trout is to break away from his mysterious captor, but first he must overcome a substantial handicap. The spring in the fly rod is really the trout's most dangerous enemy because it effectively prevents him from applying any really solid pressure. The harder he pulls, the more the rod gives. Thus, from the trout's "point of view," it all boils down to somehow getting rid of that terrible rod spring. There are several ways in which he may achieve this goal. If he can hang up the leader on a rigid object, the rod's spring will be absorbed by the snag, and he can then pull solidly against the snag. Secondly, he may be able to get the rod oversprung, or bowed so severely that it becomes rigid and relatively unyielding, much like a snag. In this interest, the trout has one potential ally, and that is the current.

To fully appreciate the current's considerable influence, find a flattened piece of waterlogged driftwood about the same size as a smallish trout, embed your hook in one side, and toss it into fast water. Lifeless though it may be, the driftwood will give you quite a fight, putting a deep bend into your rod. Trout do the same thing by using their powerful tails to turn broadside in the current, thus essentially magnifying their strength. It follows that a modest fish hooked in fast water has a better chance of escaping than a much larger one in a lake, beaver dam, or quiet pool (so long as he stays in the pool). Trout must recognize the saving value of swift water, for given an opportunity, they generally run downriver, utilizing the heaviest current they can find. But what to do about it? There are three effective countermeasures: (1) chase the fish downstream, thereby reducing pressure on the rod; (2) give him line as he goes; and (3) keep the fish out of big currents in the first place. Of these, the last plan is clearly the best, but whether the trout is capable of running down a current will depend upon the result of a matchup between his swimming power and the angler's ability to control his movements. The amount of pull the trout can generate is naturally a function both of his size and the kind of current he's in when first hooked. Angler control involves a great many factors. The fisherman will have better leverage if he's relatively close to his adversary and armed with rod of reasonable length that isn't too supple. A major consideration insofar as the amount of pressure the angler can safely exert has to do with the caliber and condition of his tippet, and to a lesser extent, the size of his hook. (Of course, it's hard to know how well your hook is embedded, and so any degree of pressure whatever amounts to a calculated risk.)

Sometimes the fisherman is simply overmatched, as I was one afternoon in the canyon of the swift Roaring Fork River, some five miles below the town of Aspen, Colorado. It was nearly 4:00 p.m. when I saw the first rise of the day in a deep pocket below a boulder near mid-river. The water was unwadeable at this point, and so I had to cast a long way from the bank and across current. Luckily, my dry fly parachuted down gently just above the previous rise ring with several seconds worth of drag-defeating slack, and a thick-bodied Rainbow took it with confidence. I got a good enough look to see that this was a member of a gang of tough 15- to 20-inch fish that frequent this water, and while he seemed securely hooked, I knew immediately that I was going to be the loser. My tippet was a slightly frayed 4X, and the fish took some 45 feet away at the very edge of a speeding, green current chute that pounded down and between two sharp-sided, tooth-like rocks. As we've said, there's just so much tension the terminal tackle can take before the leader breaks or the hook tears out, and this time the equation read: highly combative Rainbow pushing 2 pounds + extremely fast, heavy water versus a 4X tippet (somewhat worn) + a no. 16 hook, set at long range. No doubt about it, the trout was in the driver's seat unless I could somehow follow him down, but crumbling, rocky banks crowded with brush took away this option. There was just no way to keep this raucous Rainbow from running away downriver if he so desired, and he did! After sulking for a few seconds, he suddenly burst into the channel, like a fullback into the end zone, and between the jaws of the rocky "scissors." The entire episode took less than 10 seconds, and while I justifiably had a feeling of utter defeat, the outcome was hardly surprising. Trout of this size in this kind of water are odds-on favorites to escape. Indeed, during the remainder of that afternoon, I hooked three more trout, all of them large; I lost two and landed one, but only after a furious downstream chase that took nearly 15 minutes.

Once in a while, a trout will flout the rule by running upstream, as if he didn't know better. Years ago on the lower Encampment River in Wyoming, I hooked a perfectly enormous Brown that gained his freedom in this way, and he taught me a lesson at the same time. He took in broken water just above a long, lake-like pool, and anticipating that we would have it out in serene surroundings, I began to work downstream along the bank, assuming that he would soon be along. Instead the big fish took off straight upstream at a terrific clip, and into a fair current at that. I splashed along behind as best I could, but was losing ground (or water) fast when a peculiar tug came from my reel. I looked down just in time to see the free end of the line disappearing through the guides! This truculent trout was about to rip off my fly, leader, and a new line in the bargain! Managing to grab the loose end, I tossed the rod and now empty reel onto the bank, hardly breaking stride. Minutes later I caught up to the fish in a shallow flat where he had understandably stopped for a rest, trailing his 90-foot burden of line. We battled hand to jaw, so to speak, and I was winning too, for he became increasingly listless, but then I got close enough to see the Brownie's true size, and buck fever set in—a fatal case as it turned out. Losing my head completely, I attempted to drag the fish into my net through sheer force. His snout was only inches from the rim when, held hard, he merely twitched his massive head, and the fly was free. This brute of a Brown is my personal all-time "big one that got away." I'm not sure that I've hooked a fish as large since, and yet the disaster probably could have been prevented had I carried some line backing. It's no trick to splice 50 yards of strong, braided nylon to your line, and it takes up very little space on the reel spool. Backing is like a spare tire for the angler who is after trophy trout, particularly in big water.

This experience dramatically underscores the fact that the fly rod is very literally a weapon for the angler. I'm almost certain that I would have that Brown on the wall of my study today had the rod's spring been in play instead of the feverish death grip with which I held the naked line. Current is the trout's major ally, but you will become one too if you "horse" your fish by exerting so much pressure that the rod is oversprung. Horsing a trout against a current is doubly dangerous, since a fully sprung rod loses its resiliency; in this event, you might as well be pulling the fish in by hand, as I attempted to do on the Encampment. Hazardous though horsing may be, it's only natural to try to secure your prize as quickly as possible. It follows that, almost without exception, beginners need to be reminded to ease off on rod pressure and slow things down in the process of getting their fish landed. An oversprung rod is definitely a liability. Central to the dogma of "easy does it" in handling a hooked fish is the well-established fact that trout tire rather quickly under the influence of steady rod pressure even if the rod is *only partially sprung.* It's constant, prolonged tension that does the job, rather than an extreme degree of pressure. In this regard, it has always interested me to watch an old pro manage a large fish under difficult conditions. It really seems that the veterans go into a relaxed state of slow motion; the bigger the prize, the cooler they become!

An alternative method by which a trout may work out his own salvation is to anchor the leader on something solid. Just as current strength varies from stream to stream and area to area, so does the relative availability of potential snags. A favorite tributary of the Big Laramie River in northern Colorado (mentioned in the chapter on fly rods) contains fat and ferocious Browns living in a veritable jungle of willows.

Mid-summer water conditions usually call for a 5X tippet, and this makes for some real excitement, since a tangle of willow roots is seldom more than a few feet from any trout when it's hooked. Despite an absence of significant current, the Brownie's initial surge is often too strong for the tippet to handle safely in terms of effective counterpressure, and the majority hang the leader in short order. About six out of ten either snap the tippet or tear the hook out, and those that I manage to land frequently have to be unsnagged several times.

On occasion, it seems that individual trout have an escape plan already prepared. An Idaho friend tells of twice losing a huge Rainbow on the roots of a particular clump of willows near the center of a shallow slough on Silver Creek. Angry, after the second defeat he waded out and removed the dead wood. Sure enough, several days later when he hooked what he believed to be the same monster (who knows?), the fish proceeded to circle the area where the snag had been. Round and round he went for some minutes until, seeming to panic, the big trout smashed headon into a brush dam at the outlet of the slough in the manner of someone jumping through a window. Of course, he easily shed the fly, wriggling down a small channel connecting with the main stream.

I can't quite match this fish story, but a pretty Rainbow once played an even more devious trick on me. I hooked him on my side of a long, exceptionally swift channel current, and expecting my opponent to streak off downriver, I anxiously surveyed the rocky bank below me. However, to my surprise and relief, he jumped twice and then dashed directly *across* the strong flow at right angles, proceeding to skulk about in quiet shoals against the opposite bank. Now things looked easy. I could apply gentle (but tiring) pressure while strolling down to the current tail, ford the river, come back up the other bank, and finish him off in the still shallows. It appeared that this trout's instincts had played him false. I should have known better, for as I began to move leisurely down the bank, the line commenced to make a peculiar back-and-forth motion. The fish would pull hard, taking out about six inches of line, and then give it right back as if he had changed his mind. When I belatedly caught on to what was happening, it was too late for a tattered 2X tippet. The Rainbow had plastered himself against the far side of a diamond-shaped piece of shale, and was in fact sawing the leader against its edge! I waded over to examine the dozen or so pieces of shale that had fallen from an overhanging limestone cliff, and to my amazement, I found that he had chosen one with an exceptional cutting edge! Was I the victim of bad luck, or a clever trout?

Although really large trout have things pretty much their own way, it's frequently possible to anticipate and foil the escape plans of more ordinary fish. It's an excellent idea to look around for potential problems such as swift currents and snags just as soon as the hook goes home. You may be able to lead or force the trout away from them and into safer water. In other words, choose the battlefield if you can, before your opponent does. Slow, fairly shallow water with a nice clean bottom is ideal from the angler's standpoint, but regardless of whether you can herd your quarry into this kind of setting, at least maintain constant pressure on the line at all times, no matter how light. Quite apart from tiring the trout, it is important to avoid giving him any slack whatever, for if you do, your fish is quite likely to find mischief of one kind or another. It takes some experience to learn to judge just how much pressure can be safely applied to a given fish in a particular setting. As you would expect, they become progressively easier to manage as they tire, and as mentioned earlier, a rod with at least medium action can exert more pressure without becoming oversprung than a slow, whippy one. This is a significant consideration in rod selection where heavy water and heavy fish go together.

Most broken or straightened hooks and snapped tippets are caused by an over-anxious strike that creates an instant of rod rigidity. Thus, for the most part, the hook either takes a good bite and holds on the initial strike, or it doesn't. However, if you've set the hook without much force, as when the slack barely gets taken up on the strike, it may be wise to give it a second crisp but careful snap. This is especially true with larger and hence duller hooks that may not have penetrated past the barb.

An angler's position relative to that of the trout and to various sources of potential trouble is very important in the early going.

For example, the Roaring Fork encounter I described was a no-win situation from the beginning. I was a long way from a strong, freshly hooked Rainbow, who in turn was only about two feet from a current chute leading to almost certain freedom. My 4X tippet and small fly, as a team, had little chance of turning him away from his escape route.

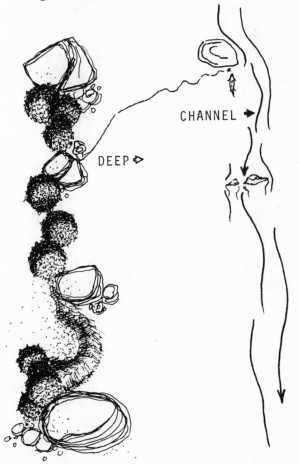

On the contrary, I could probably have kept the other Rainbow away from his shale "saw" had I foreseen the danger in time. I was below him when he struck, and could have quickly moved further down the bank, all the while exerting maximum pressure via the stout 2X tippet. In order to reach the shoals, he would have had to cross against both the rod and a tough current. This time the current would have been on my side!

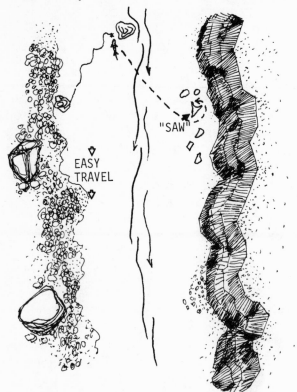

Up to this point, we have been talking in terms of a tug of war between fisherman and fish, but what happens if the trout swims straight at you? There's no way to turn back a bull-like charge of this sort. For this reason, it's highly prudent to worry about what is *betweeen* you and the trout at all times, for example, a submerged stump or swift current. Similarly, it isn't wise to stand in "dangerous" water when you bring the trout in for the final capture. Of course, the solution is simply a change in position such that the hazardous area is at an angle, hopefully one in which the direction of current flow will help you exert preventive pressure as soon as or before the trout heads for the danger zone. In this interest, it is nice if you can get downstream from your quarry, although the trout often has the same plan. If it is impossible to move below him, I'd still try to stay parallel or cross current, remembering that rod control is greatest at close quarters.

While certain types of bank provide an angler with an easy means of movement during battle, more often he will have to wade, and this means rapid maneuvering over irregular and often slippery bottoms. In my opinion, felt-soled or other fabric-soled footwear is an absolute essential for smooth, quick movement and safety, too. In fact, I seldom fish without it. I like high-top tennis shoes with this kind of sole because they are cool and light weight. Felt-soled hip boots are expensive, although there are reasonably priced strap-on sandals with good soles that fit over boots or ordinary tennis shoes. Many anglers put soles on their own gear, using commercially available kits or carpet remnants and rubber contact cement.

There are certain species differences among trout in their reactions to a hook. Rainbows are champion jumpers, sometimes throwing the fly while airborne. Although I've heard theories as to methods for discouraging their acrobatics, they don't work for me, and so I just sit back, enjoy the show, and hope that my hook stays put. Rainbows sometimes expend their energy early, shooting their wads like a boxer trying for a first round knockout. Belligerent Bows may defeat you in this way, but more often than not they can be landed if you're able to weather the storm. Browns, too, are capable of spectacular leaps, but I look for a more thoughtful struggle from them, perhaps involving a search on their part for deep snags. Dogged, hard-fighting Brookies and Cutthroat are long on strength and stamina. If of any size, they are certainly equally worthy, if less spectacular, opponents.

I rarely use a net, because they are a bother to carry, and any trout, no matter how large, can be brought to heel in docile fashion when thoroughly tired. I make an exception in situations where I expect to be way out in deep, swift water with treacherous footing. Here the net can be a sure-fingered extension of your hand when held downstream from the fish so that the current sweeps him into captivity. It's very bad practice to swipe at a trout with either your hand or a net. Rainbows in particular

106

seem to carry a spare power reserve, even after they appear to be completely whipped, and seeing the approaching hand or net, they may take off with full afterburners, catching the angler off balance with the line held tight. It's fun to watch this happen to someone else, especially when the fish runs between the startled fisherman's legs! It is awfully hard to be patient right at the end when your trout seems helpless, but a few more seconds of "playing time" can be good insurance. Remember that while trout have impressive power for short bursts, they lack long-term staying capacity, and every second of line tension builds up against them. It's possible to further hasten their submission by holding their heads up out of water on a tight line, so long as this doesn't involve excessive rod pressure.

All this advice I've put out doesn't mean that my own track record in getting fish landed is unblemished. Far from it. I've pulled some remarkably dumb tricks over the years such as tripping over retrieved line that shouldn't have been in the water or tangling the rod tip in overhead brush during the last few seconds of battle such that rod spring is totally damped out. Pulling the line-leader knot through the tip guide is another excellent way to lose a fish. The knot usually gets caught there (unless you go to the trouble of splicing your line and leader), and when the trout makes a last-gasp run, he finally has a rigid rod to pull against. Two additional landing hazards come to mind, both of which give beginners trouble. There is nothing wrong with beaching a tired trout by gently easing him onto a sloping sand or gravel bank against the spring of your rod, but be very careful about pulling a still lively fish across a shallow bar or into thin bankside shoals. Given this opportunity, he may plant a muscular tail broadside against the bottom, and with his head above the surface, deliver some solid jolts against the hook and leader. Extremely shallow water is always dangerous until the very end. Secondly, beware innocent-appearing beds of water weed. Trout will instinctively embed themselves in the soggy stuff, picking up heavy gobs of salad on your leader until, when you pull the mess in, most of the burden is vegetable. This oversprings your rod, and at the same time, the fish may be able to anchor his tail in the moss well enough to wrench out the hook. Afraid that a five-pound ball of water weed would damage my rod, I've often lowered the tip so that I could pull in the line directly. Pointing the rod tip down and directly at your quarry is always bad practice for obvious reasons, but it's better than a broken tip, and weed globs frequently come back fishless anyhow. If at all possible, steer your fish away from the green goo.

We've talked at some length about how to avoid losing good trout, and yet today, releasing them safely is far more important. Returning trout to the water unharmed should become a habit, and not one just reserved for minnows. It's best if they aren't handled at all, and so many conservationists begin by dangling small fish on a hand-held leader in hopes that the fish will fall off on their own. If this fails, I grasp the fish just behind the gill slits, *gently*, with due respect for the anatomical fact that vital chest organs are poorly protected from my grip by his soft ribs. Incidentally, I am much opposed to "gilling," that is the practice of slipping a finger into the gill slits as a means of picking up a fish. Membranes that cover the gills are far too delicate for pressure of this sort, or even the abrasive touch of a finger. If you intend to release a trout, don't gill him. Further, should your finger stray into the roof of his mouth, you will learn a painful lesson about sharp vomer teeth. If possible, I remove the hook under water, but if the barb is hard to reach or deeply set, I lift the fish out so that I can really work on the hook, and quickly too, because the trout is suffocating all the while. The little two-tined hook disgorgers that come on leader clippers are a big help, but if more than ten seconds pass, it's best to revive your patient by holding him facing upstream so that water runs in his mouth, and out the gills. When the hook is free, he should be able to swim from your hands on his own. As a youngster I can well remember tossing trout far out into the current. I was too ignorant to realize that they might drown, even in water, if stunned or just plain exhausted. Barbless hooks are certainly commendable; however, I rarely find an angler using them, and since special areas for barbless hooks aren't yet common, I would rather push the concept of careful removal of regular hooks. It may take a few extra seconds, but it can be accomplished without mortally wounding a trout. We used to be told that once hooked, most fish will die anyway. This is perfectly ridiculous. During the season just past, I kept records on several rivers in which all trout less than 12 inches must be returned by law. Of the fish I caught, nearly 25 percent had fresh hook wounds, and fully 40 percent showed evidence of older healed or healing ones. I'm additionally happy to report that a number of these trout were of legal keeping size too. Capable anglers as well as good sportsmen had evidently been at work! We must all follow their lead, for our angling futures hang in the balance.

PUTTING IT ALL TOGETHER

It's clearly impossible to summarize the complex tactics and techniques of stream fishing in any kind of reasonable fashion. Long lists of things to do or not to do hardly reflect the fascination of fly fishing and make for pretty dull reading, besides. Nonetheless, beginners naturally tend to compare what they are doing on the stream with the activities of more experienced and more successful anglers, and this really amounts to collecting lists of rules. I know I've profited by watching better fishermen at work in one setting or another over the years, and in so doing, I have identified a basic approach if not a philosophy that seems to be woven into the attitudes and actions of productive anglers. This central "theme" is efficiency, but not the kind one associates with processing stacks of paper work at the office. Efficiency in angling terms need not equate with boring detail, repetition, or the nervous stress involved in meeting some deadline. After all, many of us go fishing precisely to escape these pressures. Perhaps I can best illustrate by describing an older angler with whom I often fished in days gone by. He was neither a sophisticated fisherman, nor an unusually energetic one, for that matter, but his catches were uniformly impressive. During the course of the day, I would often find him resting on the bank, contemplating nature, and after lunch he frequently stretched out for a nap. Meanwhile, I staggered in last from the stream each evening, bleary-eyed with fatigue after a long day of water beating, only to find that he had usually doubled my catch! While I wasn't necessarily competitive about who had the best record, it was hard to understand how my friend could take life comparatively easy and still catch so many trout. We used very similar techniques and tackle, and so I concluded that his edge must stem from highly effective use of those minutes he spent in active

fishing. To begin with, he was a superb water reader, preferring detailed, broken stretches to pools. He knew that swift, apparently monotonous water is often loaded with willing trout, and equally important, he recognized that this kind of water is "Greek" to the eyes of most anglers, who can neither read nor fish it effectively. Cutting down on competition in this way was a valuable, if indirect, road to efficiency. An aggressive wader, he forsook the confinement of banks, preferring the freedom of the stream bed, where he could ferret out fish from the smallest pockets. He used upstream approaches and natural drifts in such a way that the current obligingly returned his fly to him. This gentleman was far from a fancy fly caster, but he had little need for picture-book deliveries, since he was usually right on top of his targets with short, crisp, drag-free casts. By cutting false casting to the necessary minimum, he displayed his fly in or on the water a full 50 seconds out of every minute, and by working at close range, he minimized problems with slack-line control while enjoying the best possible visibility for driving home a dry-fly hook or stinging a trout on a slack-line strike. My friend had an unusual disregard for the distinction between sunken and floating flies. In those days, we used a local brand of "two way" flies that could be fished either wet or dry, and it wasn't unusual to see him present the same fly on the top, partially submerged, and then well sunken, all within a period of five minutes! He would go through this sequence from time to time throughout the day, regardless of which presentation had been best up to that point. In this way, he eliminated the possibility of falsely assuming that either wet or dry flies *should* be best. Quite apart from this sort of on-going testing, he liked to mix occasional cross-stream and direct-drag retrieves with natural drifts, or just fussed a little with a dead-drifted fly by giving it a gentle twitch. He felt that at times, this added action seemed to provide a subtle touch of realism to the presentation. This veteran angler believed that the most productive combinations of water type, fly, and presentation could change from hour to hour, and through this technique of restless probing, he found that he was better able to stay on top of things. Most vital of all, though, my colleague had a nice appreciation of just how many presentations a given piece of water deserved. Pockets of dubious value got the once-over-lightly, or were ignored altogether, while better pieces received more attention, as appropriate. However, he basically moved right along, covering a great deal of water, and showing his artificial to lots of trout in the process. His movements were purposeful, giving an overall impression of quickness but not haste! For example, in drag retrieving a fly through a target, he would bring it back in a leisurely fashion, knowing that naturals generally proceed slowly, and gladly sacrificing extra seconds to this cause, rather than speeding ahead with a rapid retrieve.

The facets of fly fishing that can be hinged into the efficiency theme are innumerable, if sometimes a bit tangential. The major principles outlined in the chapters on water reading, figuring the float, approaching, fly casting, slack-line control, and various tackle components are all linked together in this regard. For example, upstream approaches are made from the trout's blind side, allowing one to work safely at close range. The roll cast is an easy, accurate means of putting out a fly without backcast worries. The strike/hook ratio can be a tremendous time saver by suggesting a change in pattern or hook size. A rudimentary knowledge of the insects one is liable to encounter along or within a stream provides a valuable shortcut to the selection of an effective fly, and so on. Turning to tackle, I believe that a rod of reasonable length armed with a line that will make it work in close, plus a relatively short, sensibly tapered leader, is an efficient rig. A few impressionistic fly patterns

are simpler to manage than dozens of matching patterns and yet offer general trout appeal. Weighted wets that sink neatly to the desired depth are desirable. Tying your own flies is the very epitome of angling efficiency. There are many ancillary pieces of equipment that help an angler do a better job, such as polarizing sun glasses, leader clippers, hook disgorgers, and the like, but none is so important as felt- or fabric-soled wading shoes. There is hardly any efficiency involved in falling in! Even the homely old barrel knot for splicing on fresh tippets gets into the act by saving flies, hooked fish, money, and ultimately, time as well.

A major factor in an individual angler's efficiency rating has to do with the amount of water he covers in a given period. This will be determined by the amount of time spent working an average piece of target water, and the number of targets fished. Each is an important variable, since it's quite possible to either "over-fish" or "under-fish" a stream in this regard. There are no pat answers to the question of how many presentations a certain target ought to receive. George La Branche, the pioneer American dry-fly fisher, stressed the value of repeated perfect floats over difficult trout in an effort to tease them into rising, perhaps as many as several dozen casts to the same trout. Obviously, this takes up a lot of time; however, La Branche wrote about sophisticated eastern fish, and it is my strong impression that our rough and ready western trout usually strike on the first few presentations, or not at all, particularly in fast water. This is true for both dry and wet flies. As a consequence, it is more productive if one plans to limit the number of presentations that any target receives to "several." There are certain necessary modifications and exceptions. For instance, a large, deep eddy simply can't be covered adequately with a couple of casts. Not only is the surface area too great, but in view of the depth, there is considerable total water volume as well. Bottom-dwelling trout apparently scan the upper water layers and surface film from time to time, like so many watchmen making their rounds. In this setting, it's wise to show the fly in the same area several times, since the first two or three casts may go unnoticed while the next one can bring up a good fish. It most certainly helps if you can train yourself to spot signs of trout interest *short* of a true strike. Many times, a fish will stir when a fly comes over or through his neighborhood, so that if the fisherman is alert, he will notice a glimmer, flash, or shadowy movement. Whatever it is that catches your eye, pay close attention, for it could be a tip-off as to the presence of a potential customer that may literally hammer your fly the next time through!

I kept careful records on a recent trip to the North Platte in Wyoming, in which I charted each strike against the number of floats over the target it took to draw that strike.

Floats	Percentage Of Total Strikes
First	25
Second to Fourth	70
Fifth to Tenth	5

It is evident that I would have missed three-quarters of the strikes had I limited each target to one float, but on the other hand, I was pretty much wasting my time after the fourth presentation. I spent an afternoon in the identical water just a year later under slightly different conditions, but with the same size and pattern of dry fly. This time, a larger proportion (60 percent) of the trout hit the first float, with almost no takers after the third; you can't make strict rules about this sort of thing.

The number of targets fished during a span of time is a variable that's shaped by all kinds of factors, including seasonal changes. The small stream near Colorado Springs I've mentioned in several chapters is a case in point. Swollen by snowmelt, its spring-time width reached 25 feet when murky waters swept swiftly over grassy banks, providing an abundance of cover. Hatches were skimpy, although there was a good deal of terrestrial bank food, and nymphs were plentiful. Mid-summer found a 15-foot-wide brook, running crystal clear, much lower and peppered throughout the day by an assortment of Caddis and May fly hatches. By fall, the trout were having trouble keeping wet in an eight-foot trickle you could almost clear with a standing broad jump, and they had retreated en masse to scattered pools that provided enough depth to conceal them. The shifting values and availability of the three basics in water reading could be charted like the example on page 112.

Reading the stream was difficult during May, when brisk currents plus relatively deep and discolored water obscured the bottom and combined with complex bank detail to make a "busy" picture. The trout were well spread out, and so much of the stream graded high enough in terms of reading values that I covered only a half-mile of water during an average day. The July edition was really quite different. Easy to read in comparison, holding was no longer much of a factor, while cover had become more important because there was less of it. Now the water could be easily separated into premium, intermediate, and poor areas, and I could take trout fairly rapidly by concentrating on the still plentiful high-value pieces. During the course of a summer day, I often fished a full mile, skipping short stretches of waste water, and taking most trout on my first presentation. By September, water reading had become a remedial exercise, because the trout were where the cover was; I forgot about food and holding. Pretty riffles, once filled with fish, were now likely to be barren, even in the presence of a hatch. It took me a while to realize that I should walk right by a great deal of water that would have earned a good grade except for deficient cover. However, until I learned this lesson, my late-season catches amounted to a tiny fraction of those I had enjoyed earlier in the year. It was pleasant to follow the shrunken creek bed through rustling groves of yellowing cottonwoods, but most of the water, at least 90 percent as judged by surface area, lacked adequate cover. Consequently I did a lot of hiking between stops, covering more than two miles in a day. This didn't mean I was fishing less carefully. Quite the contrary, late-season conditions demanded scrupulous care in approaching as well as precision casting, with the result that I fished relatively fewer targets, but more slowly and carefully. Thus, I found that there was nothing to be gained by trying to cover lots of water at the beginning of the year. Instead, it was better to work a short stretch, utilizing multiple floats in one target area. The same repetitious approach was much less effective during mid-season and actually became counterproductive in the fall.

It's evident that the latitude and altitude of an individual stream influence the seasonal calendar. For example, the mountains of the Gila Wilderness in New Mexico are plenty rugged, but they are also pretty "south," and not particularly high. Despite heavy winter snows, early season comes in April, while the September conditions described above are prevalent in June! Meanwhile, in the northern Rockies, the season can get compressed into 60 days (or less) between July and September, and so you have to know the area you're fishing. In addition, the annual snowpack, coupled with the kind of spring weather that happens along, determines when the earliest good fishing can be expected. A wet year (heavy snowpack plus lingering "winter" storms) can delay this happy event by at least a month as compared with a dry year. For instance, 1972 was prefaced by a subnormal snowpack and a warm, dry spring; as a result, we enjoyed fine fly fishing on the Chama River (New Mexico) during the first week of June. The year 1973, however, saw a surplus rather than a deficit of water, and it was not until the end of the second week in July that the Chama first provided reasonable water and fishing conditions.

Current strength, water temperature, and water clarity have all been discussed in one or another context, but the three "Cs," as I call them (that is, *current, cold, and color*), deserve a final look. In extreme degree, each of the three Cs is a potent factor in discouraging trout from feeding. Cold is a problem until summer really gets underway, and again following the first winter storms at the other end of the season when melting snow again releases its legacy of

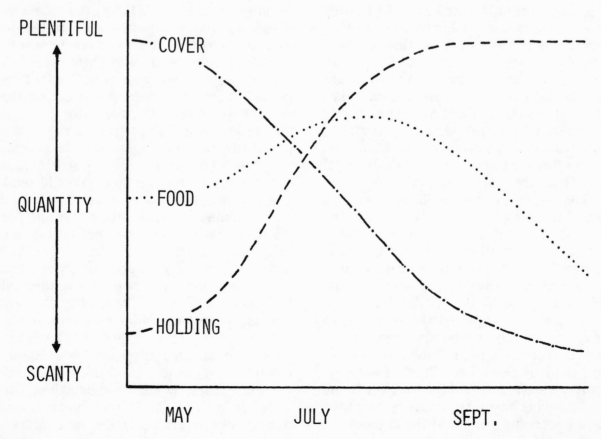

icy water into the streams below. Snowmelt is only one of Nature's refrigerants, however, for both night and day ambient temperatures are also important. Morning and evening water readings may dip under 40 degrees, thereby setting the trout's thermostats well below the active feeding range. I've found water temperature to be a reliable means of determining when and if the season is over, or has not yet begun, for one or another stream. Every trout stream has a biological clock that enables it to enter a period of hibernation at an appropriate time. Its fish, insect life, plants, and other inhabitants essentially become dormant until an "alarm" goes off, albeit gradually, in the spring. Unquestionably, maximum water temperature during the day, whatever it may be, is a major factor in setting off this alarm. To put it more precisely, when maximum recordings are below 45 degrees, it's unlikely that anyone is going to have a lot of success, bait and lure fishers included. A simple observation may prove helpful when you're faced with frigid fishing at either extreme of the season: water temperatures rise slowly during the day, probably peaking toward mid-afternoon, and it would appear that trout generally get in whatever feeding they are going to undertake at this time. By checking at regular intervals, it's often possible to see a temperature trend developing, and even to pace it. The following recordings were obtained on the Conejos River in Colorado during the last week in October. An upward swing of 15 degrees over seven hours has got to influence the fish, even as it does the wader's feet. The chart shows that I was wasting my time before 3:30 p.m., for virtually all of the action was compressed into the next three hours. This day's fishing signaled the end of the season, loud and clear. The aspen had lost their color, grass and shrubs were limp and dying, surrounding mountains were solid with permanent snow down to 10,000 feet, and a peak water temperature of 49 degrees was none too high in the first place. The skiers' turn had come!

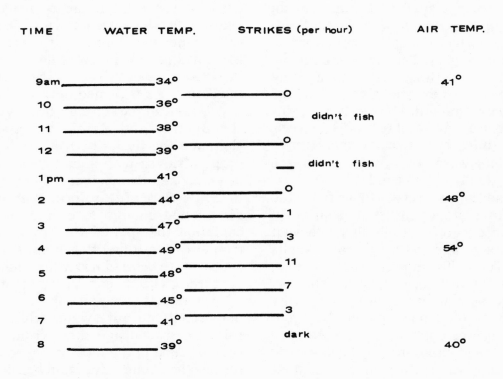

TIME	WATER TEMP.	STRIKES (per hour)	AIR TEMP.
9am	34°	o	41°
10	36°	didn't fish	
11	38°	o	
12	39°	didn't fish	
1 pm	41°	o	
2	44°	1	48°
3	47°	3	
4	49°	11	54°
5	48°	7	
6	45°	3	
7	41°	dark	
8	39°		40°

At times it's possible to guess which of several neighboring waters will be warmest. New Mexico's Brazos River is born in the northern part of the state atop a broad plateau at an elevation of 10,000 feet. Its two forks join at the throat of an impressive box canyon that cuts precipitously downward from the plateau through perpendicular cliffs to reach 8,000 feet over the course of just a few miles. The high plateau functions as a catch basin for heavy snow, just as the canyon becomes the basin's deep, shadowy drain spout. Following a September storm that deposited six inches of snow on its headwaters, the Brazos showed an 8:00 a.m. reading of 41 degrees at the lower end of the canyon. Although the day was clear and warm, I saw my first fish at 2:00 p.m., caught the first at 4:00 p.m., and finished with five, thanks to a skimpy hatch of May flies that unfolded among lengthening shadows when the Brazos reached a high of 51 degrees. The nearby Chama River has even higher headwaters in the basin of spectacular Banded Peak in southern Colorado. The pretty Chama descends via waterfalls from lofty 13,000-foot summits to wander through many miles of open valley, much of it below 9,000 feet. The Chama had been visited by the same storm, but during the summery days that followed, the sun had a good chance to work on its lower meanders. Thus we weren't surprised to find the Brazos at a bone-chilling 42 degrees the next morning, while the Chama, only eight miles distant as the crow flies, read in at an almost balmy 54 degrees! And more interesting than thermometer recordings, the warmer river offered superb dry-fly action by 11:00 a.m.!

Mid-season is pretty stable from the temperature standpoint, but post-storm roil can surely do you in. Trout strike what they can see, and too much color spells trouble. The bait clan may profit to an extent from the taste or watery "smells" released by their lures, but in really muddy water, they, too, tend to do poorly. Trout seem to become temporarily resigned to a no-see, no-feed philosophy, lying sulkily in their holding water. It's well to remember that the trout may try to make up for their period of fasting all at once when the water begins to clear. It goes without saying that one should watch for color changes rather closely, for clearing can develop over part of an hour. This is no time to be back in camp!

The annual phenomenon of the spring runoff presents the "three Cs" in concert, and fishing quality will depend upon the combination of current, cold, and color that applies. Nonetheless, at times it's hard to predict fishing quality. Several years ago, the temptation of a fine May morning led me into the Jemez Mountains for a look at the creek mentioned in the chapter on weighted wets. Snow had long since deserted its banks, and yet I hardly recognized this gentle brook. Amazingly, it had turned into a raging torrent of icy, brown water that was actually hazardous to ford. I had a pleasant day amoung the fragrant, sun-warmed pines, but I neither caught a fish nor met anyone who had. Encouragingly, a few big Stone fly nymphs clung for dear life in rare pockets of shallow water, and after recording the temperature and marking the water level, I determined to return in a week. The weather remained beautiful, and so I was disappointed eight days later when I found relatively little change. The level was down an inch or so with somewhat diminished currents, but there had been little clearing or warming. Prospects looked dim, at least until the third cast. As it turned out, that day produced some of the season's best nymphing, for Browns and Rainbows repeatedly slammed the fly on both dead drifts and drag retrieves with such verve that they often hooked themselves. In this case, the three Cs were still in force, but each had diminished enough to create an overall condition that pulled the trout's feeding triggers! I've found that it's important to concentrate on *holding water* when any of the three Cs becomes a factor, either singly or in combination. Swift currents naturally nudge trout into quiet water, while cold and roil also discourage them from actively seeking food in the currents. Typically, in the swollen Jemez Mountain brook just described, I did very little business in swift

114

currents, despite the ferocious strikes I was getting. I strongly recommend "home delivery" of your artificial when inclement conditions are at hand.

Water temperature is important, but how about the other fancy science that anglers use to predict the quality of fishing? What about the barometer, solunar tables, and phases of the moon? Frankly, I don't pay a lot of attention to these things because, like most people, I get in my fishing when I can. There's an ancient idea to the effect that trout do most of their feeding at night when the moon is full and skies are clear, at the expense of daytime anglers. In my experience, there are times when the trout behave as if there could be something to this. Otherwise, it would seem as if the formula is exactly backward with excellent fishing in the "face" of a full moon. Find enough variables to worry about, and you can take the fun right out of fishing!

It seems to me that an important part of today's stream fishing involves learning to cope with larger numbers of competitors together with associated "people problems" such as erosion, pollution, and the beaver-like proclivity of mankind to dam any sort of running water. Sadly, a good many of our larger and better-known trout waters have either been ruined altogether or made less interesting. However, a retreat to smaller streams need not mean a step many of the example situations I've used to illustrate one point or another took place in a small-stream setting. This is because the lesson in question was either learned or best demonstrated on small water. As a matter of fact, I'm not at all sure that creeks aren't better fishing schools than the roaring rivers; certainly they are more of a challenge in many ways. Indeed, little brooks have a way of putting overconfident fishermen down pretty hard. One day, I reluctantly agreed to leave the Salmon River in Idaho's Stanley Basin long enough for a family picnic, and not wanting to give up fishing entirely, I cleverly picked out a pretty little tributary stream with a primitive campground. However, when we arrived, it turned out that my wife was less than enthusiastic about watching the chil-

dren while I fished. I dutifully started a small fire, and had pretty much resigned myself to wiener and marshmallow roasting, when a devious idea came along. What if I put my youngest and liveliest son, then seven, on my shoulders while I fished? He could have fun landing them, and later we would broil our catch over the coals! I tied on a substantial fly so that he could watch the rises, and thinking ahead to his strong-arm methods of getting trout into custody, I went with a short, stout leader. Well, lunch turned out to be late, quite late I was told, and the menu eventually reverted to hot dogs as planned. After 20 minutes, Jim got deposited on the bank, the big fly gave way to a no. 18, the leader became much longer, and the tippet dwindled to 5X. Still no luck; it was becoming a matter of pride. I was finally reduced to casting from my knees, having crawled into position, before I caught and released two pan-sized Cutthroat. It would have taken me most of the day to provide enough for a meal, not because there was a dearth of trout, but on account of their extreme shyness. Approaching is almost invariably hardest in this kind of brook. Serpentine streambeds and brushy banks force one to work at close range, and trout are obviously extra spooky in thin, clear water. Fly casting is also difficult for some of the same reasons, and in addition, the angler is usually reading miniaturized detail. Instead of dropping his fly onto the crest of a six-foot channel current, he must hit a 10-inch-wide flow, and while targets may be small, there is a great diversity of closely clustered water types such that currents of different speed and direction lie side by each. Accordingly, the potential for drag in small-stream work is usually considerable, and precision slack-line casting is an essential skill, more so than on big water. Severe surface glare can be devastating unless you can change your visual angle, yet creekside brush usually hems an angler in to an extent that most options of this sort are no longer feasible. One can see that small waters are not necessarily minor league at all. Sometimes this goes for the trout that live in them, too. I've been beaten out for our family's "biggest fish" honors on more than one occasion by a youngster who was relegated to a small tributary for safety's sake while I took on the main river!

Finally, the water reading and other techniques learned on various creeks have helped me to prosper on some good-sized rivers. As a lad, I recall feeling totally lost on the broad Gunnison River in Colorado. Most of that river was one great current, water that I could neither read nor reach very comfortably with my casts. Fishing the Gunnison really wasn't much fun for me until I learned to think of the narrow strip of shallower water along the bank on my side as if it were a separate small stream. Here I felt at home, pieces of target water were clearly defined, an occasional trout rose spontaneously, and my casting efforts were at least adequate, if not polished. At times when the central river wasn't productive with deep-running lures and baits, I sometimes enjoyed better fishing than my elders. Incidentally, I'm not above reverting to these tactics today, when conditions warrant.

As I pointed out in the beginning, stream fishing is an action sport, and action things are learned by doing. It's time to leave the books behind—and get on the water!